GW00480800

The Sounds of Memory

The Sounds of Memory

Massimo Freccia

MICHAEL RUSSELL

© Massimo Freccia 1990

First published in Great Britain 1990
by Michael Russell (Publishing) Ltd
The Chantry, Wilton, Salisbury, Wiltshire
Typeset by The Typesetting Bureau Ltd
Wimborne, Dorset
Printed and bound in Great Britain
by Biddles Ltd, Guildford and King's Lynn

ISBN 0 85955 170 9

For Nena

Acknowledgements

My thanks are due to the late Aldo Satta for the hours we spent reminiscing about our youth; to Wanda Toscanini Horowitz for reliving with me so many memories of the Maestro and of the old days; to Niccolò Rucellai and Charles Gerhardt for verifying points of research; to Anthony Rhodes for guidance on some linguistic niceties; to Dr Carl H. Goldman for years of physical and moral maintenance; to Deirdre Grantley for her invaluable help; and of course to my wife, Nena, to whom this book is dedicated and without whom it would never have seen the light of day.

MF *with father*

Not far from Pistoia, just above the village of Candeglia, a winding country lane flanked on both sides by a stone wall climbs up the side of the valley. As you ascend amongst the neatly tilled vineyards the road dwindles progressively into a footpath which leads to the top of the hill. Here, concealed in part by ancient chestnut trees, stands the parish church of Valdibure. In the sacristy a dusty worm-eaten bookshelf contains a yellow piece of paper asserting my legal existence: 'Massimo Filippo Antongiulio Maria Freccia was born on the 19th of September 1906.'

My parents waited seven years for my arrival. They were staying with my mother's parents when I appeared one evening just when the butler announced that dinner was served. I was delivered in the drawing-room, and the whole thing was very messy and not as formal as desired. This happened quite a long time ago, in the country in Tuscany, when electricity had not reached the villages and there was no running water. Medical assistance was generally given by an old doctor, who for four decades had brought all the population of the neighbourhood into the world. He came from a nearby village, riding a horse at walking speed for birth delivery, trotting for strokes.

My mother got all the attention. I was placed and forgotten on an armchair. So, I believe, began the psychological complex of 'hate to disturb', the desire to be 'formally asked', and the making of 'not a pushing character'.

My photographs were never carried in my father's wallet or placed on my mother's dressing-table. They thought, 'Children, they all look alike.' I agree with them. There was no professional musician in the family (I suspect that my father always thought that music was a disagreeable noise), but my mother was a good amateur pianist and she encouraged my growing interest in music, which eventually had a disastrous influence on my academic studies.

I was six or seven when my mother came home one evening accompanied by a pale, elderly gentleman with long white hair, dressed in a shiny morning coat, carrying a black wooden case.

'The Professor', she told me, 'will be your violin teacher.' This event had a lastingly depressing effect on my father's morale.

My family lived in Florence. From my infancy I was brought up in a gloomy fifteenth-century *palazzo* in the medieval part of town, surrounded by small houses whose ground floors were occupied by blacksmiths and coachmen, who carried on their activities in the narrow streets. These neighbours considerably enlarged my vocabulary, with the result that I was thrown out of the elementary school and entrusted to the care of an English governess. She left six months later in despair, to be followed by

MF (standing) with mother, tutor and Vieri.

a long line of tutors. Then one day my brother, Vieri, and I committed an entire legion of lead Roman soldiers to the top of a stove just to watch their annihilation. The gesture was interpreted by my father as defeatist, anarchical, and subversive. A tough Dominican was placed in command of my education.

I was not sporting, but I had a sense of coordination and sports came naturally to me. I was always, however, a bad student. I adopted a passive resistance to every sort of discipline and concentration. I had instead a certain facility for the violin, and rapidly overcame the tedious stage of the beginner. When I reached the point where I could play some easy pieces, with my mother accompanying at the piano, she was in Heaven. A gift for sound and a good sense of pitch made my practising less unbearable for the rest of the family. My violin teacher, too, was pleased. I was improving steadily, although my dedication to the

MF playing the violin, with Vieri, father and mother.

instrument was not all he would have wished; but I had to contend with Caesar's *De Bello Gallico*, while not caring a bit about the campaigns in Gaul.

Studying music made me look strange to the boys of my age. I preferred playing the violin to the company of my contemporaries. I thought it was better to get used to being with grown-ups, as eventually I should have to spend a larger part of my life with them.

We always spent the summer months in the country north of Florence, in a sixteenth-century villa which my father acquired two years after my birth. This place played a major part in my life up to the age of seventeen. It was the usual Tuscan *fattoria*, with some land, a few farmhouses, and a chapel of sober architecture. The inside of the chapel was simple and austere, the only monument the tomb of the first tenant. The walls of the sacristy, at both sides of the altar, were redecorated at the beginning of the nineteenth century by two frescoes in doubtful taste, representing respectively the martyrdom of St Lawrence and St Michael triumphant over the dragon. Between St Lawrence roasting on a grill and St Michael waving a sword (he had just decapitated a Hydra), I made my first public appearance.

That summer I often played the violin during the holy service – sometimes my tutor celebrated Mass. My father very much enjoyed his company: in the evening they used to read and discuss Greek and Latin poets. Father believed that it was absolutely necessary to master etymology. A man of considerable literary knowledge, well versed in Italian, French and English literature as he was, he would have liked his son to follow in his footsteps, and was rather worried that I was dedicating three to four hours daily to music.

Life in the country at that time differed from the present day. We left Florence in June for the holidays, and we did not return until the very end of October. During those four months we saw very few people other than our guests. The village consisted of a few scattered farmhouses. One of these, on the main road, was the post office and the grocery, with an adjoining stable for the stage carriage. A fat old man used to run the business, with two daughters and a son.

The two sisters were very much alike. Both dressed in long black skirts to their ankles, oily dark hair parted in the middle, pulled back to the neck. They never talked. The elder was the postmistress, and all day long she stamped the incoming and outgoing mail. The younger took care of the grocery shop, wrapping the customers' purchases in a thick yellow paper – black olives, salami, spices. The son ran the stage carriage twice a day to the nearest city, ten miles away. The old man did not work. He just supervised and sat all day long in front of the store in shirt-sleeves, open waistcoat, an extinguished cigar in his mouth, watching the occasional traffic on the dusty road. I used to look at him with curiosity and fear. His round blue eyes peered back from between red-rimmed lids. The rumour was that in his youth he had killed a man in a brawl and had escaped to America. A stowaway on a freighter, he landed illegally in the New Continent, earning a livelihood peddling painted clay statuettes, a customary trade of his fellow villagers emigrating to the United States. Twenty years later an amnesty was granted, and he returned to Italy with enough savings to buy the grocery store. I stared at his coarse features and at the hand that drove the knife into a heart to satisfy his honour.

During his stay abroad he had acquired an Italo-American dialect. He was proud of his notion of English, and delighted when he had the opportunity to sing his favourite poem for me. Rocking his head left and right, he would tap his fingers gently on his knees as his raucous voice gave out the following mysterious words: 'Eessoh feesheeskah sellingbuy ... sellingbuy ... ' This was repeated and repeated, then with a gloating smile he would wait for my appreciation. I invariably said that it was beautiful, although I never understood what he was singing. It was only forty years later, while glancing through a collection of nursery rhymes, that I discovered the meaning of his song: 'I saw three ships come sailing by ... sailing by ... '

I often walked the three miles from the post office, climbing through olive groves on hot dry summer days. From the deep blue sky the sun poured gold on the olive-silver leaves. Sharp Mediterranean shadows branded the ground. When I reached the limit of Father's property, where the path touched the highest point and three cypresses marked the boundary, I would sit on the ancient roots, looking out over the farmhouses spreading through the plain. The tolling bells of distant churches held me in thrall. There I stayed until the birds gathered on the trees and the day approached its end. I was bewitched by the beauty of Tuscany.

Weeks, months unrolled with similarity. My parents rarely left

*Villa San Michele di Moriano: MF's father and mother at top of steps, with
MF and cook-assistant below, watched by mother's lady's maid.*

the property. Once a week neighbours were invited for tea. We
could spot the first guest from miles away by the wake of dust
left by the approaching carriage. After tea I was supposed
to appear and kiss the ladies' hands. They invariably found
me grown – I don't see why I should have shrunk – and
invariably asked me to play Veracini's *Largo* and Kreisler's
Liebeslied. Mother played a Chopin mazurka and waltz. A
handsome gentleman, after long supplication, unbuttoned his
collar, released his tie, and sang Werther's aria 'Pourquoi me
reveiller, ô souffle du printemps?', bringing tears to the eyes of
the ladies.

Meanwhile the rest of the male guests were being shown the
garden by my father, and afforded an opportunity to admire

his finest achievements in viticulture. Behind him walked my tutor, talking with condescension to the prior of the parish, a simple country priest only interested in food – a contrast to the spirituality of the Dominican. Our guests would leave at sunset, and with the departure of the last carriage our life resumed its placid routine.

At a time when in the country bread was baked at home, wine, oil, meat and vegetables were products of the farm, and farmers' wives wove their own hemp, we led a medieval life of rich solitude and serenity. To return to Florence meant to rejoin the world.

My father had decided to acquire our *fattoria* because the villa in Ardenza, where the Freccias had lived for over fifty years, had no farmland. A few fields at the end of the park were used as an orchard and were tilled by a family that had lived there for three hundred years. As they were always short of money they could never pay the rent, extremely modest though it was. On the other hand we were very fortunate to be able to recruit from among them the best and most faithful maids and menservants, who remained devoted to us and were with us until they died. Nevertheless, the upkeep of the property was too expensive for it to be used only in the summer months; we needed a self-supporting estate that would not require too much supervision.

There was another inconvenience to the villa in Ardenza. Mr Partridge, an Englishman who owned it before the Freccias bought it, had the unfortunate idea of shooting himself in one of the rooms and had forgotten to take his ghost with him. It was so attached to the place that it scorned the many efforts made to exorcise it by the local priests and the Bishop of Livorno. Even a procession on foot to the sanctuary at the top of the hill to ask the Madonna di Montenero to intercede for the cause was unsuccessful; on the contrary, Mr Partridge's ghost got very angry and redoubled its activities. I remember having heard as a

MF's uncle, General Ugo Bassi, with King Victor Emmanuel III.

child that my aunt's husband, General Ugo Bassi, a tough six-foot-five soldier who commanded a cavalry regiment, was infuriated when his bedcovers were pulled off him and the bells (used for calling the staff before the arrival of electricity) rang constantly during his visits to the villa.

As word had spread that 'one hears things', it was difficult to find a buyer and l'Ardenza remained unoccupied for some years. Eventually another Englishman, Mr Carter, fell in love with it and bought it. He made considerable structural alterations, and the noise of the pickaxe must have annoyed the ghost to such a degree that it left in disgust.

I was told by my father that it took a long time to find a suitable property. Most of the estates in the neighbourhood of Florence belonged to families who had occupied their land for centuries and had no intention of selling it. Furthermore, in the Casentino or Chianti regions the scorching heat in the summer months was not ideal for my mother's health. It was a villa in the Lucchesia that was finally chosen.

Leaving the walls of Lucca by the Porta di Borgo, following the road to the north for a few miles and turning left into a dusty country lane, you finally came to the parish church of San

Entrance to Villa San Michele di Moriano.

Michele di Moriano at the top of the hill. Impressive iron gates opened into a long straight avenue flanked on both sides by a hedge. At the end of the avenue stood the villa, surrounded by farms, each one cultivated by a tenant who worked on a medieval system called *mezzadria* – share-cropping. The owner provided the lodging, the capital to buy cattle, the farming equipment and seed; the profits were divided equally, after deducting the original investment, and the tenants, according to the traditional contract, would give the owner one turkey, two capons, eggs, and cured ham at Christmas and Easter.

The villa had been built in the early sixteenth century with the usual characteristics of that period. A double outer staircase, its grey granite baluster supported by marble columns, ran up to the *piano nobile*. The *salone* was a vast reception hall with a fireplace in *pietra serena*, yet it still had a welcoming feeling and we managed to be comfortable with our oil lamps, candles and open fires. Half the ground floor was divided into kitchen, larder, servants' dining-room and another hall, where big terracotta *orci* – for storing oil – were kept. The other half was taken up by a long tunnel-shaped chamber with huge vats on either side.

The nearest building was the house of the *fattore*, who supervised the tenants, and next to it stood the *frantoio*, where in early November the olives were pressed. This was a large room with a granite basin in the middle where a gigantic millstone turned round and round, crushing the olives. A cow provided the energy by pulling the shaft, while a farmer followed with a container ready for any eventuality when she lifted her tail. It was a biblical scene.

There were many other buildings – for storing grain, for the withered grapes selected to make a special sweet wine, for the cured hams and the seasoned cheeses – as well as handsome stables built at the beginning of the nineteenth century by a previous owner, Archbishop Volpi, who loved horses. The stalls were made of pitch-pine, and polished brass mangers were attached to the walls. The neat harness-room, with its agreeable leathery smell, was beautiful.

Walking on the Via Appia: MF's mother second from right.

Chiesina di Mammoli.

Behind the buildings a winding lane led to a little church –
Chiesina di Mammoli – built on the estate by its first owners, the
powerful family of the Sanminiati. Their crest was sculpted on
each building. One of the Sanminiati ladies died 'in the odour
of sanctity' and the legend was that she protected women in
labour. It was traditional for an expectant mother to spread her
nightgown on her tomb to be blessed before delivery. As we kept
the keys to the church in our villa, we were often woken in the
middle of the night by an excited farmer asking us to open its
doors as his wife had started her labour pains.

The front garden consisted of terraces with pots of lemon trees
gradually descending towards the orchards on both sides of the

avenue. Further off to the left a row of sombre ilexes protected us from the wind. As children we avoided that part of the garden, as on hot summer nights one could see will-o'-the-wisp. Peasants sometimes buried a dead cow or a sheep in the field below and the released gases created a flame that frightened us.

Farming methods had not changed for centuries and the farmers were stubborn and hostile to any improvement. Their lives were ruled by the Saints' anniversaries: 'For St Benedict's Day the swallow arrives under the eaves' – springtime has arrived, vegetables must be planted. San Giovanni is harvest time; on St Martin's day the new wine is tasted.

In September 1920 I was fourteen years old. Early one morning I heard a terrifying roar. It was followed by a violent tremor. One wall in my bedroom split open for the fraction of a second – and I saw my father in the next room. This was one of the worst earthquakes ever to hit Italy. The villa withstood the shock, but it had to be girdled with strong chains and firmly secured at each of its four corners as the earth went on shaking spasmodically for weeks. We camped in the garden where the horses, cattle and sheep which had been let loose kept us company. Eventually life returned to its normal rhythm.

After my mother's death my father spent his last few years at Moriano. My professional engagements kept me away from Italy, and after my father died I finally left for America. The villa remained empty, and the farm was supervised by my brother. In 1939 we received an offer for it and the estate was sold. It was a sad moment.

We often had visitors at the gate. Farmers asking for remuneration for having shot the fox that had ravaged the neighbours' chicken coops for months, showing in evidence a ten-year-old moth-eaten skin which had been used for the same purpose several times in the past. An old man from a distant village bearing a crumpled letter signed by the parish priest – with the date frequently altered – to prove that his horse had died. Barefooted monks with sacks on their shoulders grateful to receive a bushel of corn; sisters of the Passionist Order begging for alms.

We always had dogs on my father's property. The official breed was Airedale, which reigned for more than thirty years, mating occasionally with imported specimens to revitalise the strain. They were sturdy, courageous, gentle and hospitable – except to nuns. The sight of those black garments fluttering in the wind aroused violent feelings in them.

It was a torrid August afternoon: the monotonous chattering of the cicadas told one that the sun was still high. I was reading in the drawing-room when suddenly the noise of a ferocious row came from outside. Two nuns had ventured into the garden through the half-open gate, and the dogs were viciously attacking them. Gino, my father's valet at the time, managed to get the sisters into the house and offer assistance. In the country one is used to medical crises, but we had never treated nuns before.

The two ladies of the Holy Order were in such a state of hysteria that it was impossible to reason with them. The less damaged one was reciting Hail Marys at the top of her voice, while the other one was sobbing and kissing her rosary. From the torn part of her gown we deduced that the bites were on a soft part of her body and that it would be sacrilegious for us to lift her skirt.

As the blood was flowing we had to reach a quick decision. We covered the patient with a sheet while the other nun untied the intimate garments, leaving only the injured part exposed. During the medical treatment, the litany of the Saints replaced the rosary. They left with a fat donation and a bitten bottom.

On the subject of dogs, my first personal dog, years later, was a springer spaniel. I have always been fond of sporting dogs as I share their love of nature. I enjoy watching that look they have when lifting their heads against the breeze, eyes half-closed, nostrils slightly twitching.

When I selected the puppy he was the most beautiful and promising of the litter of four. I dedicated all my paternal affection to him, and planned his educational programme. He quickly mastered the tedious period of house-training, and I was looking forward to the days when we both would take long walks in the woods. Later on, when his hunting instincts were more developed, I would be able to show off his skills out shooting and he would win the praises of my friends.

Alas, I was bitterly disappointed. Of all the heroic attributes that I had hoped he would possess, only his name was left: Siegfried. He was not the rough out-of-doors type, he had a very gentle, sensitive nature. He was a calm and devoted companion; when I was working at my scores he would lie down next to my chair with his brown eyes never losing sight of me. If I raised my voice a little when talking to a friend, he interpreted it as a scolding and sat in a corner facing the wall. When I sent him out for his necessities, he would be terrified of being abandoned. He was happy on the lead – a psychoanalyst friend of mine once told me that the lead gave him the security of the umbilical cord.

When violin soloists came to my house to rehearse with me, he was restless; music did not soothe him. He only liked Jascha Heifetz, especially when he played Debussy's *La Fille aux Cheveux de Lin*, because the violin was muted. Then I gave him a rubber ball, and he played for hours all by himself, looking up in the air, balancing the ball on his nose, a trick that I have seen done only by seals in a circus. One day I noticed that he was not eating anymore. He had swallowed the ball. The subsequent operation was too much for his heart and he died.

I had just finished reading a book in bed and was about to turn off the light and go to sleep when I heard a strange noise coming from the entrance. I thought at first it was the wind but as the persistent scratching became disturbing, I decided to go down and open the door.

I was confronted by an enormous German police dog that entered the house unceremoniously and sat in the entrance staring at me. Given the size of the animal, the breed, and a set of white teeth all too visible above a dangling tongue, I decided to be prudent and after a 'Poor little doggy, you must be hungry', I went to the kitchen to prepare him a substantial meal.

He voraciously gulped a large bowl of meat, then sat down again staring at me. I took a good look at him. He was a particularly beautiful specimen, but surprisingly wore no collar. Not having much confidence in unknown dogs, especially of that race and size, I opened the door and invited him to leave. As he did not move, I locked him up in the entrance and went back to bed. It was 1942, in Cuba; at that time I was living in Miramar, a lovely residential section of Havana not far from the sea.

The following morning I ventured into the entrance with sensible caution. He was in the same position in which I had left him the night before; his eyes stared at me without emotion. All attempts to discover his origins were fruitless. The announcement in the daily papers, the efforts by the police to find the owner, were totally unsuccessful. I adopted him to avoid his being destroyed.

It was not an easy task as I had never before had to contend with so strange an animal. The only affinity he had with the canine race was an insatiable appetite. The usual affection that a dog has for the person who feeds him – an occasional wag of his tail, or a casual bark – was alien to him. I thought he might respond to commands given in Spanish or English, but I had not the slightest success.

He used to leave the house in the late afternoon every day and walk to the sea, sitting on a reef until sunset, staring at the horizon; he then returned home for his bowl of meat. Our relationship was very formal and we both minded our own business. He disliked abrupt movements – they would make him dart at my arm, immobilising it, though without damage to anything but my nerves. The postman, who had unsuspectingly entered the house, once had the dog's fangs at his throat until my arrival.

In Cuba we all knew that German submarines used to enter deserted inlets on the island to refuel and that members of the crew went ashore to buy provisions for their ships – in the United States when some German sailors were taken prisoner, ticket stubs for a cinema in Miami were found in their pockets. Then a friend of mine, Colonel Fred Sampson, who was the Military Attaché at the British Legation and an expert in training that type of dog for the Army, told me that some U-boats carried Alsatians on board. The mystery was solved. I began to give him orders in German which he promptly obeyed, but I always treated him with due respect.

He stayed with me for a year and a half and he returned to the sea every afternoon, scanning the horizon until sunset. One day he was sitting in his customary place on the reef. He seemed more nervous than usual. All at once he plunged into the water and swam out to sea. I called and called, but he did not heed my shouts. I watched his head disappearing in the distance. I never saw him again.

During my childhood, parents were little concerned about freeing us from complexes. When reprimanded we were often slapped. At luncheon or dinner with our parents we were forbidden to speak. Our nurseries did not have the cheerful atmosphere of their American equivalent – no pink or light-blue furniture, comic cartoons of animals, Bambis, jumbos or teddy bears embroidered on the baby's towel. My brother and I had a room that would have given the creeps to a hangman. We slept on brass beds. The rest of the furniture was dark mahogany, which provided a further depressing mood for our adolescence. The walls were covered with faded wine-coloured damask and

Vieri and MF.

adorned by a single painting of large dimensions. The lateral effigies, blackened with age, gave great prominence to the two central figures: an emaciated Christ in agony dangling from the Cross and a weeping Magdalen at his feet. The twelve-foot ceiling was decorated with an allegorical fresco of three ladies representing Faith, Hope and Charity. Faith was the most terrifying, waving a torch, while glaring at a cloud with staring eyes. Hope did not look at all confident; wrapped in a green mantle, with a sad expression, she leant on an anchor. Charity sat between the two of them, encircled in a haze of vapour, her right hand upholding an enormous breast, the nipple of which coincided with the centre of the ceiling where a three-inch long pipe was still attached. This ancient residue of an old-fashioned gaslight made her appear as if she were blowing a whistle with her bosom, while her left hand bestowed a bun.

My mother's name was Porzia de' Rossi, and she came from an aristocratic Pistoian family. In the thirteenth century her ancestors owned the land from the slopes of the Apennines to the plain, and they were the lords of Pistoia. But in the course of five centuries they lost the land and the power; by the time my mother was born, all that remained was a lovely villa with some farmhouses.

On her father's side, her grandmother was a de' Pazzi, an ancient Florentine family of Crusaders, murderers, and a saint. Pazzino de' Pazzi and the Tuscan Crusaders were the first to storm Jerusalem in 1088. As a reward Geoffrey de Bouillon gave him the family arms – five crosses with two dolphins – and three flints from the Holy Sepulchre, one of which, during Mass on Easter Saturday in Florence, sets fire to the tail of a dummy dove loaded with gunpowder. This symbol of peace, with flames gushing from its back, slides on a wire from the high altar of the cathedral to the middle of the square to set off the festive fireworks.

The murderous side of the family was less spiritual but more practical. They decided to kill the Medici, even though Guglielmo de' Pazzi was married to Lorenzo il Magnifico's favourite sister, Bianca (which subsequently saved his life). The conspiracy was cleverly planned. High Mass, when Lorenzo and Giuliano would bow at the elevation of the Host, was reckoned to be the right moment to stab them. Giuliano was killed but, unfortunately for the de' Pazzi, Lorenzo escaped through a door in the sacristy. He took revenge by having some of the de' Pazzi hanged in the Piazza della Signoria, while others were banished from Florence.

Over the years the de' Pazzi curbed their murderous inclinations, and even improved their manners; they reverted to a certain spirituality. At the beginning of the seventeenth century there was a saint in the family – Mary Magdalen de' Pazzi. Her body never decomposed, and is still kept in a church under a glass case. The pillow where she rested her head at the time of her death was preserved in one of my cousin's chapels, until, during the Second World War, an American GI purloined it to make his jeep seat more comfortable.

While my grandfather's family swung from crime to sanctity (an intellectual female scored additional points in the fifteenth century by giving birth to the Italian poet Torquato Tasso), my grandmother's family, the Rucellai, included rich banker patrons of the arts. One of them, Giovanni, commissioned Leon Battista Alberti to design the façades of their *palazzo* and of the Church of Santa Maria Novella. His son, Bernardo, a great scholar, married Nannina (Lucrezia) de' Medici – another sister of Lorenzo – and they had a son called Giovanni who became an eminent writer and historian. All this looks like a pedigree of good behaviour, but my great-grandfather married a descendant of that Conte Ugolino della Gherardesca of whom Dante said in his *Divine Comedy*, 'Più che il dolor potè il digiuno' – 'Then fasting got the mastery of grief', which implies that he ate his son out of hunger when they were both imprisoned in Pisa.

The Rucellai at amateur theatricals.

As far as we can trace it, there was a Freccia family living in the tiny village of St Ilario Ligure around the 1600s. St Ilario consisted of a few small white or pink houses built on a slope, brooded over by the parish church. In the square, attached to the church, was the seat of the municipality, the governing body of the 280 souls of the village. It was a long white house, with permanently closed green shutters. Over the entrance door an oval emblem bore the inscription 'Municipio'.

Years went by with the same monotony, the only diversion being an occasional funeral or the annual procession on the feast of St Ilario. Then, in 1803, an event took place which shook the sleepy community. The priest, returning from his monthly visit to the Bishop of Genoa to report on the behaviour of his

29

parishioners, brought the news that a native St Ilarian, Antonio Mangini, a rich merchant who had been consul-general and diplomatic agent of the Genoese Republic in London, had died intestate. Now the next of kin were being sought.

After a farewell Mass celebrated by Don Gelasio, Lazzaro Freccia, my great-grandfather and a nephew of the deceased, surrounded by the entire population of St Ilario, took his leave and stepped onto a *calesse* to venture over the tortuous and dusty road to the port of Genoa. The ship for London was ready to sail.

Antonio Mangini had lived for many years in London. His business had flourished and he had accumulated a large fortune; he became so respected in the City that the proud Republic of Genoa, 'La Superba', appointed him official representative of his country. Now his numerous friends received his nephew warmly and made him feel at home.

Alas, there was another claimant. A young lady called Maria Mangini Brown declared that she was Antonio's daughter. She had married a gentleman from Baltimore and was living in America. Although no proof could be found, a special jury eventually accorded her legitimate status, and she became the heiress.

Lazzaro had no alternative but to return disappointed and empty-handed to St Ilario. Not long afterwards he moved to Genoa, where he founded an import-export business and married the attractive daughter of a Count and Countess Fontana.

From the paintings still in my possession, his mother-in-law seems dull but kind; his father-in-law, on the other hand, looks like a pretentious ass. A white wig over a self-satisfied and supercilious face, a sword hanging from his left hip, lace protruding from his sleeves, makes him look pompous; the right hand holding a bank draft of £200 suggests both arrogance and, worse, bad taste.

Over the years the Freccia family grew prosperous and

prominent. The eldest son, Filippo, my grandfather, bought the villa in Ardenza a few miles south of Leghorn; the second became a notable judge of the court of Genoa, and the third, Luigi, was a landowner who married and lived with his wife in the north of Italy. The only sister was called Maria Augusta.

My grandfather was a patriot. He married into a family of intellectuals who were fighting for the unity of Italy. They secretly met with Giuseppe Giusti, Giuseppe Montanelli, and other conspirators to plot the removal of Ferdinando of Bourbon from Naples and Sicily, the Hapsburgs from Tuscany, and the separation of the Vatican from the State. All staunch royalists, they were devoted to the House of Savoy. Vittorio Emanuele II was already King of Piedmont and Sardinia; with Garibaldi, he was about to defeat Pius IX and take over Rome.

If my grandfather's political dream had already triumphed, the merchant bank he had founded in Leghorn was about to collapse. Day after day he climbed to the top of the tower of the Ardenza villa in order to scan the horizon with his telescope, hoping to see a sign in the distance that would announce the arrival of the three cargo ships he was awaiting from abroad. It never came. A storm in the Atlantic had sunk all three. He was all but ruined.

Soon afterwards he happened to read in the daily paper that Maria Mangini Brown, the daughter of Antonio, had died in London intestate on 21 December 1871, and that once again the Crown was asking the next of kin to come forward. As the eldest brother, my grandfather was selected to go to London to establish his claim. His wife and children remained in Ardenza and he sailed alone for London where he settled in a house in Bayswater.

The size of the inheritance – almost half a million pounds in 1871 – was such that it aroused the greed of numerous false relatives, forgers and swindlers. Leading newspapers carried daily reports on the progress of the ensuing lawsuits. The litigation lasted for many years and was widely written up as an example to the public of the dire consequences of dying intestate.

Poets' Fountain, 1875, taken by MF's grandfather.

The matter ended with an appeal to the House of Lords which terminated the dispute by confirming the judgement of the Vice-Chancellor, Sir Richard Malins, in the High Court of Justice, declaring the Freccias the sole legitimate heirs.

After the death of her husband Maria Mangini Brown had lived for the rest of her life in a house at the foot of Park Lane. She was intelligent and cultured, with a great love of poetry. In an urge to beautify London she commissioned Thomas Thornycroft to create a monument in memory of the English poets. It was to be erected in front of her house in Hamilton Place. On a circular pedestal were marble statues of Chaucer, Shakespeare and Milton. On the lower tiers were seated bronze figures of three muses – Comedy, (Thalia), Tragedy (Melpomene) and History (Clio) – while on the summit a winged gilt figure of Fame was blowing a trumpet. Thomas Thornycroft's son, (later Sir) Hamo, assisted his father by carving Shakespeare, Comedy and Fame. Maria Mangini Brown died before it was finished, and my Freccia forebears had to pay £5,000 for the monument, which was called, quite simply, 'Poets' Fountain'. Inaugurated on 9 July 1875, it was finally removed in February 1949, having deteriorated sadly, not least from bomb damage during the Second World War.

Over a century had elapsed when my wife and I spent a week-end in Derbyshire as guests of our friends Reresby and Penelope Sitwell at Renishaw. When walking in the park my attention was attracted by a statue standing on a pedestal. It represented a gilded figure of a young girl with wings, the left leg slightly raised, a wreath on the left hand, with her right cupped in front of her face. I thought I recognised her. On my return to London I studied the photograph taken by my grandfather of the monument in the 1870s. Indeed the gilded girl at Renishaw was the Fame of the statue. Reresby told me his uncle, Sir Osbert, had bought it and that it had originally stood in Hyde Park. I told him that the trumpet was missing from the girl's cupped hand. Since then Fame has been given a new one.

Studio set-piece photograph showing MF's grandfather, Giulio de' Rossi, with MF's grandmother (Maria Rucellai), with children (left to right) Beatrice, Girolamo, MF's mother, and Maddalena.

My mother was beautiful, with exquisite features and captivatingly melancholy eyes. She was very delicate, and after my younger brother's birth her health became precarious. She had been educated at home with her sisters and they all played the piano, sang, and spoke French and English. In her last few years, however, she could no longer play the piano, and became interested instead in literature and theological studies. She also became very pious, and prepared herself for death. When it came, it was as gentle as the burning down of a candle. A heavy silence pervaded the house.

She had been happy with my father, a handsome man, smartly dressed and an amusing raconteur. He had read law at Geneva University and Oxford, was a competent watercolourist, and always carried a sketchbook in his pocket to draw a belfry or some scene which stirred his fancy. By profession he was a solicitor – most of his clients came from the English and

34

American colony in Florence – and eventually he followed with vigour in his father's footsteps in squandering the remnants of the consul-general's fortune.

My mother did not travel much, particularly latterly, except for a pilgrimage perhaps to Lourdes or to the shrine of St Anthony of Padua. My father, coming from a family of enthusiastic travellers, was – for those days – well travelled; while his

MF's mother, c.1910.

eldest sister rode a bicycle from Calais to Leghorn in 1885 to advance the cause of female emancipation. She had earlier run away with an Englishman (whom she eventually married) and settled in London, where she joined literary circles and wrote for newspapers and magazines.

At the beginning of June my parents gave a yearly ball, generally timed to coincide with my mother's return from Switzerland where she regularly spent three or four months in Divonne to take the cure for her delicate nervous system. My father was the sole organiser of the event, and my brother and I followed the preparations excitedly. Two of our gardeners from the country would arrive with plants and flowers to decorate the conservatory where the orchestra was to be placed, and we would ask after our summer playmates, the farmers' children. Then the upholsterer made his annual appearance to take the fitted carpet off the Nile-green polished surface of the dance floor, while two pensioned servants were recalled for the occasion to deal with more delicate matters, such as washing glasses stacked up in a cupboard since the year before, or removing the tarnish of hibernation from the grander silver. The final details reached perfection – last touches to the tablecloths, servants straightening the candles in the chandeliers to ensure that the glass rings would catch the drops of wax.

I remember once when my brother and I, at that time five and seven, and not invited to the ball, were allowed to stay up a little longer so that we could make a tour and admire the results of all the efforts. Then we went to bid goodnight to our mother while she was dressing. We were terribly impressed by her beauty. After a kiss each on the forehead we were sent to bed.

But we had in mind a totally different plan. After putting on our pyjamas and extinguishing the light, the idea was to sneak out of our room at the appropriate moment and tiptoe down a corridor to the not-too-distant conservatory and hide near the

The ballroom, Florence.

orchestra in the shrubbery of azaleas, palms and gardenias. Here we would have an excellent and undetected view of the ball.

After what seemed an interminable wait in the bedroom, I heard the first sounds of revelry. I tried to tell my brother that the moment had come, but he was sound asleep. Not being able to wake him up, I had to leave by myself for the hideout. It was an ideal place from which to have a good view of everything without being seen. The two gardeners, immaculately clean and shaven, in livery and white gloves, were assigned to the entrance to take the gentlemen's coats and hats and the wraps from the ladies, to whom they then gave the *carnet de bal*. I could see my father in the distance, dressed in a tail coat and white tie, with my mother standing next to him, greeting the guests.

The white and gold ballroom, with its glittering crystal chandeliers reflecting the warm light of the candles, made a splendid setting. Long ostrich-feather fans in different colours, matching the ladies' gowns, added a gentle movement to the scene. Footmen circulated with champagne glasses on silver trays, while the orchestra played incessantly. The occasion must have been too much for me. I fell asleep.

When I opened my eyes it was daybreak. My mother had retired, my father was still saying goodbye to small groups of guests while footmen were snuffing out the candles. He then complimented the butler on the splendid work, and retired to his room. I retired to mine.

I knew my father left the house punctually at ten in the morning. I was anxious to wish him goodbye and I went to his room. He was almost ready to leave. He straightened up his tie, took off the band that kept his moustaches twirled up, caressed both cheeks with the right palm to feel if he was properly shaved, slipped on his coat, and after a final tug with both hands to his lapels, left his dressing-room through a corridor leading into the entrance hall. I followed him. On a table in the centre of the room two bowlers, one grey, and one black, neatly aligned, awaited his choice. It fell on the grey and after a quick additional brushing it was handed to him by Piero, the faithful valet, with a pair of grey suede gloves and a malacca walking cane.

He told me to go back and do my homework. I watched him walking down the baroque decorated staircase leaving a wake of lavender scent. Piero blew into the polished brass mouthpiece of a speaking-tube connected with the porter's lodge, and warned him to open the gate. Then Piero quietly closed the door. We had returned to normal.

During the First World War my father, who was too old to join the army, made his war effort the organisation of La Casa del Soldato, in which soldiers could rest after battle. These homes not far from the front were supported by civilians who provided food, books and all possible comforts. A young Englishwoman, Teresa Hulton (later Lady Berwick), and Monsignor Costantini (later Celso, Cardinal Costantini of the 'Propaganda Fide') were his enthusiastic supporters. His Royal Highness the Conte di Torino, a cousin of the then King of Italy, was not only my father's personal friend but also a patron of the organisation, and an important liaison with the army. He was very tall and immensely distinguished; he always carried a walking cane, and the cut of his civilian clothes was such that he could be immediately spotted as a cavalry officer. When people recognised him in the street they raised their hats. He would acknowledge the gesture with courtesy.

One day he was visiting my father and I, uninvited, entered the room. He immediately stood up with the extreme politeness that keeps ordinary people at a distance from Royal Highnesses.

'I suppose that you are the young musician?' he said.

'Yes, Your Royal Highness,' I answered.

'Do you like music very much?'

'Yes, sir,' I said.

'Are you going to be a professional musician?'

'I hope so, sir,' I replied.

'Very well, very well, my boy. I trust that you will become a Verdi ... or perhaps a ... Beethoven.'

I remained speechless. Seventy years have gone by and I still cannot think of an answer to that.

My mother's younger sister married a gentleman from Bologna. He belonged to an aristocratic family which, originally from Ancona, moved in the sixteenth century to the more cosmopolitan city of Bologna. He was a cultured man, with no business commitments and a large fortune at his disposal. He had the leisure to study, attend social gatherings, be President of the Società del Quartetto, and to be a member of the board of the Teatro Comunale for the annual opera season.

He was a good amateur pianist although sometimes his rhythm suffered from what he called 'rhapsodic interpretation'. When he played four hands with my aunt, they had conflicting opinions. She objected to his 'rhapsodic interpretation' which she defined as plain lack of knowledge of *solfeggio*. This insulting remark invariably provoked a violent altercation which ended with the lid of the Blüthner grand piano being slammed and a few hours' silence in the house before they started their playing again. I was very fond of both of them and delighted when they invited me to stay.

Bologna had a great musical tradition. The Liceo Musicale, named after Padre Giovanni Battista Martini, was founded in the seventeenth century, and several musical geniuses – including Mozart – had studied there. The Italian première of *Lohengrin* took place in Bologna and the city prided itself on being the only Wagnerian centre in Italy, performing a Wagner opera every season.

I was fourteen years old when for the first time I was allowed to travel alone to visit my uncle and aunt. The trip by train at that time was an adventure. At the stop in Pistoia, after the first uneventful thirty odd kilometres, the passengers were suddenly seized with growing tension. Crossing the pass over the Apennines was a daring undertaking. To lighten the load of the train, the rear carriage which was reserved for the local passengers from Florence to Pistoia was detached to make place for an extra engine, a very short chubby contraption without a tender but with containers on both sides of the boiler for the coal supply. It pushed while the other engine pulled.

During these proceedings the passengers took the opportunity of rushing to the station restaurant to buy supplies of mineral water, *panini* and, if available, smelling salts for the ladies. Then, to the violent slamming of carriage doors and shouts of 'Godspeed' from the people who remained behind, a green flag waved by the station master gave the order to the driver for departure. The train panted out of the station in a cloud of white steam.

The thirty-four tunnels separating Pistoia from Bagni della Porretta, the highest point of the pass, kept the passengers busy opening and closing the windows. As the train approached a tunnel, the leading engine gave a warning whistle, echoed immediately by the engine pushing from the back; but none of this prevented thick black fumes from filtering through the coaches, making the ladies and gentlemen look like the darkest Ethiopian tribe by the time they reached the summit.

Bagni della Porretta is a small village with miraculous waters that cure arthritis and other ailments. Since the railway was diverted in the twenties to a faster route, the place is out of fashion. It stands astride the mountain pass and the air, because of its altitude, is light and fresh. Every train stopped there to get rid of the rear engine that had provided such valuable help and to give the passengers a chance to breathe again. The train then resumed its journey, gliding happily towards the plain of Bologna, a landscape totally different from that of the austere Tuscan countryside, with green meadows neatly divided by straight lines of poplars, rivulets, terracotta-coloured farmhouses – the first taste of the fertile Po valley.

A hand of cards at the Bosdaris' Villa Russo, Bologna: MF's father and mother with friends, c. 1903.

My uncle was waiting for me at the station, and I was promptly informed of the coming musical events. A concert conducted by Willy Ferrero was to take place a few days later. I had heard the name of Willy Ferrero ever since my childhood. He had been a child prodigy and had conducted symphony orchestras all over Europe since the age of seven. He was now fourteen, my age, and I looked up to him with awe and envy. His father, a showman in a circus, lived in a trailer, camping near his ring and travelling throughout Europe with his family.

This gentleman appeared in a most successful act. After ten white ponies, ostrich feathers on their heads and a lady trainer in command, had jumped, walked on their hind legs and knelt to the audience, Signor Ferrero made his elegant appearance – black cape lined in white silk, top hat, white tie, tailcoat and monocle. He was about to conduct the Intermezzo of *Cavalleria Rusticana* with an orchestra formed by eighteen hens lined up in a pen, facing a revolving cylinder concealed by fake flowers. The starving chickens had their eyes glued to the revolving roller, so that they could peck up a grain of corn which corresponded to a musical note. The result was the performance of Mascagni's Intermezzo. The trick was ingenious, and its success gigantic: the act had made him famous. When, after two or three years, his renown started to dwindle, the hens, I surmise, ended in a pot; and his attention then fell on his seven-year-old son.

The boy was intelligent and precocious. Brought up in a crowd of theatrical people – clowns, Chinese jugglers, acrobats, trainers who put their heads into lions' mouths – he had no inhibitions. As a gift for music ran in the family, the father decided to make a conductor out of him. He taught him popular symphonic pieces by ear, let the boy's hair grow long enough to be marcel-waved, dressed him like Little Lord Fauntleroy, hired an orchestra and put him on stage in front of it. The boy had a natural sense of rhythm and was an instantaneous success. His father, to glamorise further the miraculous gifts of his creation, inserted false notes into the orchestra parts in order that the boy, warned in advance, would correct the mistakes at rehearsal, furthering the legend about his exceptional ear. The child prodigy was exhibited everywhere. Showered with presents, acclaimed in every country, he became an international celebrity. Unfortunately when the legs became too hairy and the shadow of a beard too visible, he had to abandon his Lord Fauntleroy suit and his fame receded. Notwithstanding, he had a nostalgically faithful public right up to the end.

I saw him last in the Fifties; he died, an alcoholic, shortly afterwards.

Versilia, the northern part of Tuscany before you enter Liguria, is a flat gentle land that stretches from the Alpi Apuane towards the sea. The mountains in the distance yield the famous marble of Carrara; I still remember in my early youth the sight of two or three pairs of oxen dragging a cart laden with huge blocks of marble down to the jetty and the waiting sailing ships.

With Ugo Bassi at the seaside.

My brother and I, aged five and seven, would go down in the morning to the sea. We were accompanied by a *tata*, a nanny very formally dressed in an ankle-length black skirt, half-boots buttoned up to the top, a blouse with long sleeves, starched collar, and a yellow straw hat with a big black bow. We wore one-piece down-to-the-knee short-sleeved bathing suits, and we pushed a wooden wheelbarrow loaded with pails and shovels. Large white linen slouch hats protected us from the sun. We swam, built castles with wet sand, watched them destroyed by an unexpected stronger wave, and waited for our parents to arrive.

It was at midday when they made their appearance. I can still see my mother in a long, pleated cream dress with a whalebone collar in tulle, the bodice loosened at the bosom and swept down to the tight broad silk belt around the waist. A hat with a stuffed seagull on top of it added a slightly improbable touch of marine elegance.

My father, escorting her, would be impeccably dressed in a

white drill suit, wearing a Panama hat with the brim lowered on one side, and carrying a black walking-cane with a silver handle.

Years later I accepted an invitation from my childhood friend Amerigo Gondi to see the place again. He lives for part of the year in a charming small villa in Forte de' Marmi. After lunch we walked towards the sea. We did not talk too much about the past; it was more of a silent reminiscence.

The vast beach was deserted. It was a late October day. Rows of empty cabins painted in pink and blue and yellow dotted the greyish sand, with here and there an overturned rowing boat.

'Do you remember my *tata?*' Amerigo asked me.

I said I did. ·

'Do you know what she said when we brought her here from Florence the first time? We waited eagerly to hear her reaction but it took some time to come. She looked about her in silence. Finally she said: "Certainly the sea is wide, but the Arno is longer." '

On the beach at Forte de' Marmi.

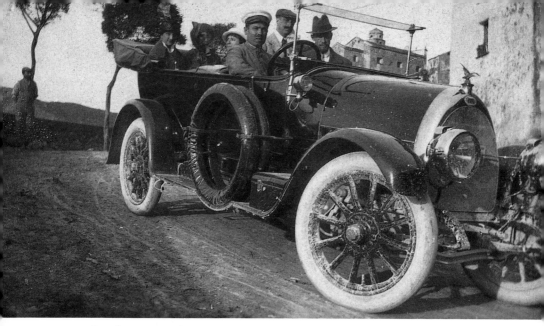

Family outing in the Fiat, Lucca.

An important thing happened at the beginning of the First World War: my Russian great-aunt came to live with us. We divided our flat into two in order to accommodate her, and she shared the expenses of the heating – the main reason for this co-existence. She moved in on a rainy November day, followed in procession by her household. A towering personality who would have obscured Chaliapin's entrance in Boris's coronation scene, she led the way wrapped in a long red velvet tunic with matching slippers. A triple string of pearls dangled to her knees; in her left hand she held a globe with a roosting parrot, her right hand was outstretched in a regal blessing. Next came her two maids carrying furs, birds' cages and a square alligator-leather bag where the jewels were kept which represented her portable – and dwindling – treasury. A whiskered butler holding six Pomeranian dogs, a footman with a monkey, and other members of the household laden with samovars, silver warming-pans and stuffed dogs (ancestors of the current Pomeranians) completed the menagerie. The installation did not take very long; every detail appeared to have been planned in advance. The stuffed dogs were placed under a Bechstein piano delivered the day

46

before, glowing embers were poured into the samovar to warm the water for tea, and my aunt finally sat on an armchair from which she did not move for the duration of the war, except to sit on the piano stool a yard and a half away. She suffered from cold, and insisted that every window should be hermetically closed, nailed, and sealed with thick felt bands to prevent draughts. She was intelligent, witty, original, sensitive, exceptionally musical, unusual, and her life was eccentric.

Not trusting the Italian daily papers, she regularly sent a servant into Florence to pick up gossip, to wander along the streets on the trail of the latest news and bring back a vividly detailed account of a tragedy, a brawl or a feast. As an organ needs air to feed the pipes, she was constantly longing for suffering to keep her heart's wounds bleeding, for stirring events whereat to weep for mankind's sorrows, or to cheer with exultation.

To me, her Slav musical complexity revealed a new world. For hours she would sit at the piano, pouring outbursts of emotion into Tchaikovsky or Anton Rubinstein. A rare feeling for harmony made her indulge in modulations, relish voluptuous chords of the Ninth, find peace and comfort in Schumann's *Romance in F Sharp* or ecstasy in Brangäne's singing from the turret in *Tristan*'s second act. Her deeply emotional feelings, the introspective bent for renunciation, abandon, romanticism, stirred my juvenile subconscious and stimulated my curiosity about a new world of experiences. Brought up by my mother in the rigorous classical tradition, concerned with the simply proportioned and restrained style of Vivaldi, Corelli, Viotti and Tartini, I was disturbed by her lack of proper phrasing and her sentimental indulgence. On the other hand, her vivid sense of colour and drama stimulated me.

In a quasi-oriental setting – icons with burning candles, Persian carpets hanging from walls, heavy curtains in a deep red damask always drawn, lampshades covered with shawls adorned with tassels, and collections of snuff-boxes and photographs of the Imperial Family scattered over the tables – her faithful

47

The Russian great-aunt and MF's great-uncle (not her husband).

devoted friends, mostly Russian refugees, gathered in the after-noon for a cup of tea. French was the official language, and they only spoke Russian when the Russian Patriarch was visiting.

During the four years she lived with us, I paid her daily visits. I would wait for the last visitor to leave, then sneak into my aunt's drawing-room where the air was still bluish from the smoke of cigarettes. I was rewarded first with left-over pastry, and then she would recount stories of her youth in St Petersburg, meetings with Tchaikovsky, Rimsky-Korsakov, César Cui. She used to read to me Chekhov's short stories, plays by Andreyev, Turgenev. She unveiled a new horizon on literature.

Her friends all had a strong individuality, like characters in a play, each with a precise role. A distant cousin in her thirties, silent, pale and emaciated, always sat near the parrot's cage, sewing countless tablecloths. Others took their place around a bridge table, keeping an ear on the general conversation, or listened to a loquacious gentleman (ex-member of the Duma) relating the latest misdeeds and horrors of the Bolsheviks, while the Prior of the Orthodox Church, attentively following the vivid description with a grimace of repulsion, would cast a rapid glance at the frightened listeners, and drawing a deep sigh would whisper in Russian 'Góspodi pamílu!' – 'God have pity on us!'

These singular people, engrossed in an illusory world of their own, concerned in the first place by the loss of their country, their fortunes and their social status, defeated by their fate, appeared to me like an amusing literary creation, a contrast to the gloom of the war.

The one who made the deepest impression on me was the Rumanian Prince Michail Ghika. He had come as an exile to Florence in 1880 when he was fifty. He rented a splendid villa in the hills, hired a staff of fourteen servants, and decided to wait. Expecting at any moment to be recalled, one of the first things he did upon arriving in the city was to place a standing order with Thomas Cook & Son for a first-class compartment on the Orient Express going east. Small and chubby, with an enigmatic face, a hooked nose and two round bags under his light green eyes, he looked like an owl. He was smartly and almost affectedly dressed.

Methodical in his habits, he left his villa every afternoon in an elegant two-in-hand for a cup of tea in the city. Diffident about the Italian concept of hygiene, he had instructed his valet the first week after his arrival to deliver to each of a few selected tearooms a set of china to be used for the princely visit. After sipping his tea and purchasing a few ounces of chocolate drops, he paid a visit to my aunt before returning to the villa. He never mixed with the Florentine aristocracy; he rather fancied the foreign colony, and occasionally received transient members of the European royal families.

One day he received a letter from his bank in Paris informing him that his income had diminished considerably, and that his expenses had to be curtailed. He immediately notified his staff of the misfortune. He moved into a less sumptuous villa, some servants were dismissed and his two-in-hand sold, but he could still enjoy his afternoon drive in a small brougham and his normal cup of tea in his precious china. He was kept informed of the political developments in his country by some back numbers of its leading newspapers, but still his devoted courtiers gave him hopes for his return.

More time elapsed, more financial upsets dwindled his revenues. With the turn of the century, new ideas stirred unrest and rebellions, wars and revolutions changed the map of Europe. He was now old and forgotten, his fortune spent. Living on a small allowance from some relatives, he had moved into a noisy third-class hotel in the centre of Florence. His health was failing, he sat all day in an armchair next to the window to have a glimpse of the world before paying his usual visit to my aunt.

One afternoon he heard some shouting: a mob waving red flags, carrying portraits of Karl Marx and Lenin, were marching in the street below. After some reflection, he summoned his valet.

'André, we are living now in a new world, a democratic world. From now on do not call me Altesse any more, just Prince.'

The news from the battlefield was grim. Father kept us aware of how slow and distressing trench warfare was, placing small flags on a map to mark the recently conquered positions. Mother helped in the Red Cross, but her frail constitution forced her eventually to stay at home to knit for the soldiers and supervise our education.

The Caporetto breakthrough caused a gap in these little flags, a wave of confusion in the nation, and a serious quarrel between my aunt and my father. The latter, a man of deep patriotic sentiments, brought up in a liberal family, whose ancestors had fought for the unity and independence of Italy, was offended by a tactless remark that my aunt had made about the courage of the Italian Army – 'A lot of damn cowards!' During the heated debate an antique Chinese vase was knocked over, relations were severed, and the flat's connecting doors sealed. This incident upset my surreptitious visits to my aunt, and to reach her now I had to sneak through an elaborate course of ups-and-downs within the servants' quarters, from which I had been banished. To retain some loyalty towards my parents I never talked to my aunt about it, and she never inquired how I managed to cross the boundary.

She fascinated me, irresistibly. She stirred an emotion that was different from any I had experienced among people of my own country. Her amazing lack of inhibition, her combination of art-lessness and mysticism, made my family seem dull and conventional by comparison. Her love for Holy Russia was not inspired by the usual sense of patriotism, such as we all feel for our own country, but by a profound mystic devotion to the 'mystery' of the Russian people. Her total disregard for the conventions gave her a certain freedom. She dressed in rich velvet tunics, and was indifferent to all rules of fashion. In her drawing-room she would cheerfully juxtapose a bag of onions to a jade collection because it was the driest spot in the house. She was gentle yet cruel, she loved her servants and she whipped them. Her sentiments went far beyond the ordinary limits of emotion. Her sense of guilt drove her to repent for the burden of Mother Russia's sins. I was mystified when she did things that I could not understand. I later discovered that her Russian complexity was just primitive.

Throughout my childhood I was on the whole happy, thanks to the affection of the grown-ups with whom I associated through my interest in music; but I felt a sense of loneliness in the company of my contemporaries. Not being able to talk to them about my emotional life, I kept an impenetrable secrecy about my sensibility. I joined their parties and their games, but never entered fully into their lives. With my increasing interest in music, and consequently extended contacts with older people, I widened the gap with boys of my own age. I was easily teased

Neno de' Rossi, husband of the Russian great-aunt.

because, for instance, I preferred tea to chocolate, or because I spent a long time looking at sunsets. The sound of bells plunged me into a profound melancholy, and they still do to this day.

I had a morbid complex about death, encouraged by my aunt's depressions. A Florentine funeral in the late evening, the light of gas lamps, the ancient Brotherhood of Mercy robed in black surplices with a rosary for a belt, their hoods drawn over their faces, carrying torches, following the black standard adorned by a skull and crossbones, left an indelible scar on my youthful world and I believe influenced my interpretations in later years. I remember, when still very young, conducting Beethoven's *Eroica* for the first time, with the New York Philharmonic, the consideration and respect given by a famous critic to my treatment of the Funeral March. I don't think it was the overall conception of the work – I was much too young and inexperienced to conquer its magnitude – but the intrinsic approach to that particular movement which projected a feeling that stirred the orchestra and the public.

On 3 November 1918, Italian Armistice Day, my father and my aunt, both in tears, embraced one another. Friendly relations were resumed. But shortly after, with the same display with which she first came into our home, my dear aunt left. I did not see her often, since her new flat was some way off. I was grieved when, a year later, she died. The Russian funeral service, the singing, moved me deeply. All her friends were present, each carrying a lighted candle. Their genuine sorrow brought a feeling of reality to these strange characters and their poignant little world. My brother and I were taken to the church with a black band stitched around the sleeve of our left arms. The open coffin lay in front of the altar surrounded by innumerable candles and a profusion of flowers. Her body wrapped in one of her familiar velvet tunics, her eyes half closed and a faint smile on her lips, gave the impression that she was trying to remember a pleasant dream. She did not have the distant look of the dead; she seemed alive but in a new world, pleased by the new experience.

The servants, in tears, knelt around her, praying. The remainder of her fortune was left in a trust, the income of which would provide for their lifetime pension and for the six dogs assigned to each one of the staff with a special provision for their maintenance. My brother and I eventually inherited the money and a few personal objects, snuff-boxes, watches, albums of photographs, and a silver samovar, her faithful companion since her youth in Russia, which still lives in my drawing-room.

Only a few years ago, while I was going through some old papers, I came across a diary which my aunt had kept from time to time. Well over a quarter of a century had elapsed since her death. I saw her under a new light, divested of theatrical 'slavism', nevertheless disclosing a profound human awareness, resignation, tolerance and goodness. Her kindness was a natural element, and an end in itself. Her death is no longer a wound which is difficult to heal. Today she is alive, she is part of my being, for I cherish her memory.

The exodus of the Russian aristocracy at the beginning of the Revolution enlarged the populations of Paris and Florence. Not having had any real academic training beyond a perfect knowledge of foreign languages, imperative in a social world, the men would take jobs sometimes as taxi drivers or doormen, the women as seamstresses. They had no resentment; on the contrary, I suspect they enjoyed the new life, the self-abasement, the self-inflicted punishment for having in the past lit cigarettes with rouble notes. Those who had managed to export their family jewels sold their diamonds and tiaras, and kept their usual eccentric life- style.

A great-uncle of mine met on one of his trips to Paris a beautiful young divorcée. He married her and took her to Florence. In my youth, in a Catholic country such as Italy, a divorcée was not received. The beautiful bride, in spite of her very noble lineage, got the cold shoulder.

She was intelligent, with a vicious tongue. Her powers of retaliation were venomous. She decided that the most wounding gesture of spite would be to disfigure the heraldic colours of her husband's family emblem. The coat of arms consisted of diagonal lines in gold and blue slanted from left to right; on top a rampant lion on a red field. She mixed the gold and blue and with the resulting pea-green brew she ordered the *palazzo* to be redecorated and all the furniture repainted, not even sparing a grand piano, a 1912 De Dion Bouton automobile or the footmen's livery. The battle with the family never ended. To give a further shock to the conventional Florentines, she published a book, *Les Mémoires d'une Cosaque*. If the literary qualities are not transcendent, the descriptions of her travels through the Russian steppes are both horrifying and amusing. The account of the pogroms is hair-raising, counterbalanced by the tale of splitting a water-melon while travelling in a carriage on a hot day and lifting her skirt in order to sit on it to cool off. I did not see much of her because she was too social, but I occasionally dropped in for a cup of tea and a good laugh.

In my youth I listened eagerly to my uncle's tales of life as a diplomat in the East. I do not know how true they were, but I recall much enjoying his tiger hunts on elephants with the maharajas of India, his adventures in China, the golden temples of Indochina. What impressed me most was when he once went on leave and returned to Italy with King Prajadhipok and the whole royal family of Siam as his guests. In Florence, in those days, we were not used to seeing exotic people. We had very many eccentric characters among the English and Russian colonies, but none from an alien world. We had only one Negro, employed as a publicity stunt to operate a lift in a department store. He was jet black and dressed in a bright red frock-coat, with a fez embellished by a blue ostrich feather. When my brother and I misbehaved, we were taken by a nursemaid into his

Uncle Girolamo de' Rossi　　　　*Vasco Magrini*

presence for a warning: 'Look here, if you're naughty again, he'll eat you up!' We were terrified by the black man, but the slanting eyes of the monarch and his retinue filled us with reverence and fascination. I had seen photographs of the ceremony of his ascent to the throne, dressed in lavish costume and adorned with the splendour of the royal orders. It set fire to my youthful fantasies.

From early days I had a passion for aeroplanes. When I could escape from my violin practice I would jump on my motor-cycle and go to the Campo di Marte in Florence to watch Vasco Magrini working on one of his aircraft – strengthening the frame, tuning the engine, anything to improve his aerobatic stunts. He had distinguished himself as a pilot during the First World War and won several decorations for bravery. After the war he built himself a hangar at the Campo di Marte, bought old ex-service planes and started his career of barnstorming. He would go from city to city, preceded by the advertisement 'Oggi si vola' – Today we fly' – and for a small sum of money would take adventurous spirits up for a ride. He would give a display of the most daring stunts – 'falling leaf', spinning, diving vertically to a few feet from the ground, flying upside down, rolls, looping the loop. I saw him fly his little plane under one of the arches of a bridge over the Arno, skimming the surface of the river.

He was a small man, blond, wiry and indomitable. We never spoke to each other and I wondered what he thought of the silent young man who was so interested in watching him at work. Then one day he asked me if I would give him a lift on my motor-cycle. He had an appointment and was running late. Next time I came he would repay me with a flight. I told him to jump on the pillion.

The following afternoon I went to the aerodrome. He smiled when I entered the hangar, and threw me a leather helmet and a pair of goggles. 'Come on,' he said, 'I'll take you up.' He helped me into the cockpit and strapped me tightly into my seat.

If I thought I would have a pleasant flight enjoying the beauty of Florence from 2,000 feet, I made a mistake. For twenty minutes he went through all the aerobatic tricks that had made him famous. The world was spinning around me and when we landed I was so giddy I could not walk straight. He asked me if I still liked flying. 'Yes,' I said in a feeble voice.

Years later I met Charles Lindbergh in Switzerland and we talked at length about flying – the evolution of civil aviation, the new inventions and the radical changes that had taken place since my youth. He said with nostalgia: 'The decline of flying started with the closed cockpit and the self-starter.' I thought of Magrini and that flight in Florence, and I half agreed.

I was seventeen when I asked my father to receive me in his library. I wanted to talk to him about my future. Having thoroughly rehearsed how to approach the subject, and prepared for all sorts of conflicting arguments, I calmly sat down on an armchair near his desk. The letter my father was writing kept him busy for a while, and this gave me time to go over once more the salient points. I was elaborating my speech when I noticed my father's eyes staring at me. Caught unawares, I stammered 'I do not want to be anything but a musician. I am considering entering the Conservatory of Music.'

A long silence followed my brief statement. I was expecting a violent reaction to my words. My father suddenly rose, and while setting some papers in order on his desk, said quietly how deeply perturbed he was by my foolish decision, how much I would eventually regret the step I was about to take, and how preposterous the idea was of a youngster of good family choosing music as a profession. He then left the room, and I remained pondering. He did not refer to the subject again, and I abided by my decision.

I entered the Conservatory in the class of theory and composition at the beginning of the term, and soon found the course in counterpoint and fugue dull and uninspiring. I paid no more attention to it than was necessary to enable me to pass the examinations. Instead, I concentrated on violin studies, expanding my still limited knowledge of chamber music, and making new acquaintances, for I was in contact with an entirely new world.

At that time Ildebrando Pizzetti was director of the Conservatory Luigi Cherubini. Pizzetti, an important exponent of a movement abandoning the theatrical *realismo* of Mascagni, Leoncavallo, Puccini, Zandonai and Giordano, had had his early operas, *Fedra* and *Debora e Jaele*, already performed at La Scala under Toscanini's direction. He was a well-established composer. In my opinion his musical message was more important in his operas than in his symphonic productions. In his form of operatic expression the music never became the slave of the libretto as in nineteenth-century operas, but always had to remain of equal value to the drama.

Florence: MF's father's study.

The incidental music he wrote for d'Annunzio's *La Pisanella* made him famous. D'Annunzio, with his usual panache, baptised him 'Ildebrando da Parma', just as Claude Debussy was elevated to 'Claudio di Francia' when he wrote the incidental music for d'Annunzio's *Martyre de Saint Sébastien*. The first of Pizzetti's compositions that I ever conducted was *Three Preludes to Oedipus Rex*, a juvenile work which in my youth I thought modern and controversial. But his music is basically boring. Although he wrote for voices (chorus) in a masterly way, the texture of his orchestration is dull and sombre. Toscanini, besides conducting his operas, fostered his orchestral music, performing all over the world the *Concerto dell' Estate* and *Rondò Veneziano*. Notwithstanding, his music never became popular and the international critique never considered it modern.

Six months after I had entered the Conservatory, Pizzetti was appointed director of the Milan Conservatory and Alberto Franchetti took his place in Florence. Franchetti, also an operatic composer, belonged to a school more inspired by the Germanic style. He wrote a few operas – the most important of which are *Cristoforo Colombo*, *Asrael* and *Germania*. The latter was performed by Toscanini at La Scala. Incapable of teaching or of imparting knowledge, he remained as a figurehead and our class was switched to a more academic young man, Vito Frazzi, who was struggling to put to music a 'King Lear' on a libretto by Giovanni Papini.

My mother's precarious health, one of the main reasons for our moving from the centre of Florence to a small villa on the outskirts, inhibited my musical activities in the house. We were no longer permitted to make any noise, and her feeble constitution did not allow her to play the piano. There was a garage belonging to the house, and it was here that I had to concentrate all my activities and here that I acquired the experience which led me to my profession. I liked that big room. I fixed it up with some old pieces of furniture, a broken-down sofa, a few chairs, an iron stove and an upright piano; a wooden board on a trestle was my writing table. I felt free: I felt myself a grown-up man, no longer subject to restraint. I could ask my friends to visit me. I was facing my future.

With the collaboration of Conservatory students and amateur musicians anxious to play ensemble music, we went every week through compositions for small orchestra, unfamiliar in a city deprived at that time of a symphony orchestra and where the gramophone was still new. On certain occasions, when the group became too large, I, as the leader, had to stand to be seen, in order to guide them and keep them together. For the first time in my life I was conducting.

In later years I have frequently been interviewed and invariably asked how I came to be a conductor. I often noticed a look of disappointment on my questioner's face when I could not offer a more dramatic explanation of the beginning of my career.

I have never had a lesson in conducting. I had to teach myself. I learnt largely from rehearsing chamber music and from watching other conductors at work. I profited more from their shortcomings than from their qualities. As a string player, I had a naturally 'easy' right arm, a gift that allows an orchestra to play comfortably, and I took advantage of the benevolence of my companions to experiment with a profession for which I was rapidly growing an irresistible longing. But my score-reading was poor, my experience limited, and my psychology nil. I conducted by instinct, and I eventually realised that it was a difficult art which could only be mastered through torment.

I met Luigi Dallapiccola at the Conservatory in Florence, and for several years we became inseparable. He lived in a boarding-house not far from our home, visiting us daily and often staying for meals. He had a prodigious memory, a caustic sense of humour, and a formidable will-power. An accomplished pianist, he used to practise for hours in my studio and to him I owe my acquaintance with a large and varied piano literature which might otherwise have eluded me. Had he not been blessed with musical genius, his wit would have made him a good critic. His love of music was obsessive, his playing tumultous. Although short and disproportioned, with a large head on a small body (always preferable to the contrary), his flashing eyes made him handsome. During the long walks we took together by night through the deserted streets of Florence, I could only admire his eloquence, imagery and keen sensibility. His critical understanding of the Italian contemporary composers already revealed a personality determined to find a new form of expression.

Italy of the Twenties, dominated for decades by Verdi's 'verismo', gave no sign of a musical renaissance. Ottorino Respighi's tone poems were the last manifestation of the moribund Romantic movement. Malipiero's shapeless symphonies and Pizzetti's operatic contributions did not entirely satisfy the young. Puccini's realism pleased the masses as much as Mascagni's with his *Cavalleria Rusticana* and Leoncavallo's *Pagliacci*. Casella, the best-known internationally among contemporary Italian composers, brought a considerable impetus to Italian artistic life, guiding the young into a more challenging musical world. I was very fond of Alfredo Casella and I always felt he had a genuine liking for me. He had numerous and eclectic talents, but his real genius lay in creating a modern Italian school of *pianisme*. I remember when everyone in Rome heard the story of Casella's encounter with Mascagni. Casella had just returned from the United States, and was boasting that he had conducted so many concerts there that he had been able to buy an automobile. He told Mascagni that not only had he played his own music at all his concerts but also the Intermezzo of *Cavalleria Rusticana* at each one. Mascagni retorted that now he knew the explanation of the automobile – had Casella played nothing but his own works it would have been a bicycle.

Stravinsky's *Les Noces*, thoroughly tonal primitive folklore, made a strong impression when presented in Florence by Alfredo Casella; but the event which shook the city was Schoenberg's *Pierrot Lunaire*, conducted by the composer. This inventor of a new and complex world of sounds was boorishly received. A restless noisy audience disturbed the normal unfolding of the performance, and the ordinary listener did not realise that he was in the presence of the man who was warning composers to revise their musical thinking. A few followed with interest, among them Giacomo Puccini; others giggled.

The concert was given at the Sala Bianca in Palazzo Pitti in a regular series presented by the Amici della Musica. The Sala Bianca, a rectangular ballroom on the first floor of the royal palace, soberly decorated in white stucco, was a splendid, elegant setting for chamber concerts. Puccini's visit was unexpected. He drove from his villa on the lake of Massaciuccoli near Lucca just to hear *Pierrot Lunaire*. He sat in the first row, his coat folded over his knees, listening attentively to the performance, indifferent to the scoffing of the audience. I don't know how much he enjoyed the music, but I felt his deep interest in Schoenberg's controversial new system. In later years, although his music is quite different from that of Schoenberg, I always felt the influence of that performance on Dallapiccola.

A group of us would meet and talk each week in the houses of various friends. One of them, a singular man in his late thirties, lived alone in the loft of a twelfth-century tower arranged as a study. After climbing up a musty spiral staircase, we eventually reached the top landing which led directly into a studio. The room was lit up by one slit on each side, through which we could see the moist roofs of Florence. Odoardo Zappulli had been born in Paris, the only son of a good-natured Neapolitan painter and an austere aristocratic Dutch mother, and he moved to Italy after graduating from a Swiss university. The room's furniture, in somewhat random arrangement, suggested considerable travels in the past – some German pieces, a Dutch coal stove, an English butler's table, a grand piano, an out-of-order cuckoo clock, worn-out oriental carpets; then a few of his father's paintings of northern nautical scenes, a sailing-ship model, an old compass.

He greeted us cordially, rubbing the palm of his right hand over the back of his left. Pale and dry of skin, his slightly twisted mouth seemed to give him a permanently sarcastic smile. His eyes were bright, almost feverish. He never worked; he had no ambitions. He lived on a very small income that gave him freedom. His vitriolic tongue lent spice to a discussion, and misery to the person drawn into an argument with him. After serving a cup of tea, he sat in his usual armchair, lit his pipe, and asked some tricky question to lead the conversation into his favourite topics – music, philosophy, religion. As an atheist, he would debate brilliantly to prove that God is an illusion, and he would tear to pieces all Christian ethics. Schopenhauer was his mentor, conscience in men was the only reality. He loved Bach, but his real passion was Wagner's *Tristan and Isolde,* which expressed his pessimistic philosophy. He knew the opera by heart; the score was always on the piano, generally open at the second act's finale: 'The land that Tristan means, of sunlight has no gleams.' There he remained for the rest of a long lifetime, like an old falcon perched at the top of his tower, true to his beliefs, serene, grieved by mankind's foolishness, his eyes still flashing with the old fire, but compassionate at heart.

I always had a passion for the theatre. Touring companies used to stop in Florence for two or three weeks, with a few plays on the bill. The beginning of Pirandello's irrational theatre caused a great stir, and Pitoeff's company brought to Italy from Paris an unknown style of acting. I recall, too, having seen Zacconi in Ibsen's *Ghosts* – a most realistic interpretation after he studied for months in a clinic the symptoms of progressive paralysis in syphilis. I thought it wonderful. Eleonora Duse in Ibsen's *The*

Lady from the Sea left a memory of a pale, expressive face and a beautiful voice still vivid in my recollection.

I took a job as an apprentice at the Opera in Florence. I was delighted to mix with an alien crowd, to learn the way in which a performance grows from the earliest piano run-through, the first shapeless orchestra rehearsal, into a vital finished performance. The spring season would last three months, and a considerable amount of operas were announced on the bill.

My first acquaintance with the theatre was in Umberto Giordano's opera *La Cena delle Beffe* ('The Jest'), embarrassingly banal music for a sanguinary Renaissance melodrama by Sem Benelli. My various duties ranged from playing the celesta and glockenspiel in the orchestra pit to rushing backstage and helping, with the aid of a harmonium, a buxom prima donna to stay on pitch while singing in the wings. I had no idea of how incredibly stupid and ignorant Italian singers were. Their lack of musical knowledge made the rehearsals at the piano exasperating and kept the performance in constant danger. Their only concern was to captivate the audience with effects, drawing disturbing applause during the unfolding of the performance.

In the Twenties, in Italy, the theatre did not have the respectability of today. Companies mustered at random, strolling singers and actors offered a Bohemian atmosphere to a world of make-believe, living in hotels and boarding-houses, travelling from city to city, lured by unscrupulous impresarios. Outwardly they may have seemed well-defined characters, but on closer acquaintance they were revealed merely as hollow composites of the numerous roles they had portrayed in their careers. Their life was the stage; they indulged themselves in the ephemeral favour of a fickle public. I watched their absurd vanity with amazement.

The conductors' mentality was not far above that of the singers. Trained in their youth in the Italian melodrama, they imparted a superficial but effective dramatic impact to some performances – when contending, for instance, with the character of Floria Tosca, or with Verdi's panached warriors, or with the sentimental vicissitudes of a slut on her way to New Orleans. But it was a talent that brought an incongruous sunshine into Wagner's nebulous gloom, a fleshy materialism into Melisande's symbolism and a Rossinian bonhomie to Mozartian classicism. I was longing for a more spiritual expression, a more intimate perception. I was divided between a passionate love for the music itself and a literary fascination with the stage.

My curiosity about the theatrical life was such that I was willing to waste precious hours in discovering more about it. I joined the performers for meals at nearby restaurants. I had forced my retiring nature to appreciate their crude jokes, their thunderous laughter, to find their gossip absorbing, to enjoy their easy camaraderie. I stayed up late at night listening to their experiences amid the noisy clatter of the knives and forks. I tried to be jovial, and not to betray my discomfort.

At that time the art of stage direction was not developed as in the present day. Movement on stage was primitive and un-coordinated. Unruly tenors and prima donnas, determined to get the centre of the platform for their arias, would fight viciously for it. A curious pockmarked man was in charge of instructing the chorus how to move. He had no imagination nor sense of composition, so the plastic arrangement of the figures was frequently unbalanced. He was short and clumsy, with long arms, yet convinced he was graceful. Once at a performance of *Boris Godunov,* to give elegance to the Polonaise, he decided to take over the role of the Polish nobleman dancing with Marina. At his appearance, clothed in an outsized embroidered tunic and dragging a sword, next to a soprano twice his size, a wave of hilarity swept the audience. He thought it was his charm which caused the stir.

My most pleasurable diversion was to watch the prompter from a hole in the scenery. He was a middle-aged man, thin and liverish, permanently sucking a liquorice tablet which blackened his tongue. He never mixed with or talked to anyone. He scarcely even mumbled an acknowledgement to the doorkeeper when collecting his mail. After hanging up his coat, he went straight to the prompter's box to wait for the performance to begin. As soon as the footlights were turned on, however, and the curtain raised, his face and body suddenly came to life. His mimicry was superb. Enunciating every word, his mobile face acquired the most vivid expression. His left palm was outstretched as a warning not to sing without his cue (Italian singers rarely knew music; they learnt the part by ear), while with his right forefinger he directed every word, nodding if his instructions were attentively obeyed. At a mistake on the part of a member of the cast he would lose his self-possession: his face would colour, he would stare at the culprit and stick out his liquorice-coated tongue, thrusting both arms in his direction, index and little finger extended in a magic gesture to expel the evil spirits. The performance over, he left with his usual indifference. He would buy the evening paper around the corner, and lose himself in the nightly crowd.

Three months passed rapidly. The season came to an end. The company dissolved hastily a few minutes after the last chord died away, and I was left alone in the theatre. The red velvet curtains were drawn, dust-sheets covered the stalls. I could see the vastness of the hall from the depth of the stage. A lonely lamp lit the centre of the platform. I walked around: the prompter's box was taken away, the flats were leaning against the walls, the scenery was neatly packed ready to be shipped to another theatre. On my way out I passed the doorkeeper's lodge. The man was eating a loaf of bread cut in two, with some salami in it, a bottle of wine next to him. With his mouth full he could not answer my goodbye.

As I walked out into the night, the air balmy with the scent of linden flowers, I had a strange feeling of apprehension that I might not be suited to the profession I was yearning to begin. I dreaded having to admit to my father that it was all a mistake, that I felt uneasy in the theatrical world, that my desire to become a symphonic conductor could not be achieved in a country where music was circumscribed by Italian melodrama. I needed reassurance. Was I critical of a Bohemian world because I felt insecure in such surroundings? And would the theatre not lose all its charm in a bourgeois respectable world? An Elizabethan touring company, William Meister's group – was it not the mysterious romantic disorderly life that fascinated me? Was the Italian melodrama the real theatre? I was gripped by an inexplicable anguish. I was walking faster and faster, my heart was beating rapidly. When I arrived home the lights in my father's study were on. He was awake, waiting for me, a grave look on his face. I sat next to him, and he remained silent for a while. He then seized my hand and told me that the doctor had just left – my mother's health was causing serious anxiety.

I am deeply grateful to a friend who came to live in Florence to study at the university. Eight years older than I and well travelled, Aldo Satta kept me up to date on events abroad. He had enough money to live on, and he could afford to attend the various European art festivals. Tall, smartly dressed, wearing a monocle, he seemed more like an Austro-Hungarian cavalry officer than a scholar. He was not a conversationalist and did not help much in a social gathering. He did not exactly stammer, but his delivery was halting. Although a cynic with women, his gallantry was impeccable, almost with a touch of old-fashioned courtesy which seemed particularly attractive to them. Extremely reserved, he never talked about himself. Only several years later, while sunbathing on a Mediterranean beach, did I discover that during the First World War he was wounded by machine-gun fire and decorated for bravery in action.

He spoke French, English and German fluently, and besides having a keen interest in literature, he truly loved music. He talked to me of books, of authors I did not know – Arthur

Photograph of Massenet, inscribed to MF's mother, Paris, 1897. The music is from Werther.

Schnitzler or Jacob Wasserman, whose *Maurizius' Case* and *Etzel Andergast* I enjoyed very much at the time, though after forty years I find they fare less well. He told me to read George Bernard Shaw, Virginia Woolf, D. H. Lawrence. Returning from a trip to Berlin, he brought me news of the artistic world in that city – three opera houses, symphonic orchestras, playhouses, a resplendent intellectual life reflecting all sorts of literary trends and political aspirations. The young Wilhelm Furtwängler, at the head of the Berlin Philharmonic, surpassing the heights attained under Bülow and Nikisch; Bruno Walter's concerts, the Singakademie offering impeccable performances: Bach's B Minor Mass, *The Passion*, Handel's Oratorios and Beethoven's *Missa Solemnis*. The opera houses ... Kleiber now promoting new music at the Staatsoper after having strengthened the old repertoire; *Wozzeck* a success after the historic first performance on 14 December 1925; Busoni's *Doctor Faust*, Prokofiev's *Love of Three Oranges*; Richard Strauss conducting his own operas; the Staedtische Oper reviving forgotten works of Verdi's early period; Klemperer at the vanguard of the Krolloper, new stage directors revolutionising traditional settings, stirring up discussions and often scandal. Novelties ... Hindemith's *Cardillac*, Stravinsky's *Oedipus Rex*, Schoenberg, Kurt Weill.

Aldo conveyed to me the essence of this spectacular intellectual life. He talked at length about new movements in the theatre, of Jessner, pioneer of a style anti-naturalist, anti-illusionist, exclusively turned toward inner expression, as opposed to that of Reinhardt who maintained the tradition of polished psychology. The predominant literary movement of the Twenties included men like Kaiser, Sternheim, unusual new works by Toller, Bronnen, Hasenclever, and the mysterious Ferdinand Bruckner, bold and fascinating, shocking the public with *Krankheit der Jugend* and *Die Verbrecher*. He told me about the new works by Bertold Brecht at the 'Junge Bühne', whose formula of *Verfremdung* was not yet promoted to a system, but was already recognised as a sign of social rebellion.

70

The unforgettable hours of chatting until early morning influenced the course of my life. I was deeply conscious of my ignorance and the lack of system in my studies. My inability to concentrate on subjects which did not interest me at that particular moment made my education superficial and full of gaps. I knew my shortcomings and I decided to learn by taking advantage of my natural gift for listening. My father did not oppose my wish to travel; he only objected to my going to Berlin, and suggested Vienna as a more suitable place. He thought of the Austrians as the Southerners of the Teutonic race, and more congenial to a Latin temperament. A little money inherited from my aunt gave me complete freedom, and I started out on my own. It was my first journey abroad.

I arrived in Vienna one September evening. My father had arranged, through a distant cousin of my mother living in the city, to reserve lodgings in a modest *pension* suitable for a student. The trees on the Ring were still thick with leaves, and strolling passers-by were enjoying the warmth of a late summer day. A cab left me at the front door of a huge grey building where plates on either side of the entrance declared the tenants' names – mostly doctors, dentists or solicitors. The Pension Theresianum, it said in broad letters, was on the first floor. An unbending young maid with spectacles, after inquiring my identity, ushered me into a large drawing-room. I could tell from the subdued reek of food and beer that it was also used for meals. The girl retreated backwards from the room, staring at me as if I were some expected delivery it had fallen within her duty to unwrap. Left alone, I observed the furniture, checked the make of the grand piano, noted the plaque under the antlers that recorded date and place of some poor creature's Waterloo. Then there was a trampling on the floor above, followed by a fine rain of plaster and the unmistakable sound of the *pension*'s owner hurrying to receive me.

Baron Eberhard von Wächter (father-to-be of the famous baritone) was a gentleman, an officer in the Austro-Hungarian

Army during the First World War. After having lost his fortune he converted his flat into a boarding-house to make a living. He was tall and corpulent, spoke excellent French and possessed a great deal of charm. He took me to my room, informed me of the habits of the establishment, and left me. The same girl who had opened the door brought me a tray with some cheese, salami, brown bread and an apple, withdrawing this time with a reassuring smile.

The following morning I went for a walk, and it was not by chance that I found myself standing in front of the Opera House. There were stage-hands carrying scenery from an opening in the back. An outgoing backcloth with the vivid inscription 'Corrida de Toros' informed me that *Carmen* had been gored by Don José the night before, and an incoming wicker basket containing an emaciated bloodstained head suggested that *Salome* was on the bill for that evening. A poster hanging next to the stage entrance carried the names of the cast, and with emotion I read, in small Gothic lettering, that Richard Strauss was guest conductor.

The house was sold out, but I fortunately fell in with a young American student who was trying to sell a ticket. I bought it for a price far above my means and awaited the performance with mounting excitement. I reached the Opera House early, ahead of a feverish public. Then the theatre was suddenly full, and the orchestra had begun their tuning. The dimming of the lights brought silence. Complete stillness, suspense; everyone's eyes converged on the orchestra pit. Richard Strauss mounted the rostrum, and with a slight nod acknowledged thunderous applause. I was expecting an exuberant personality, dramatic gestures to drive his musicians through the tumultuous pages of the score. But his movements were composed, calm, almost detached. An impassive gaze in the direction of the brasses would unleash a stormy crescendo, a benign glance to the strings would calm their ferocity. He was like an unruffled trainer in a cage of lions, certain to emerge without a scratch. He brought the performance to an overwhelming finale. After the last crashing chords he shook hands with the leader and left unperturbed, avoiding the customary appearance on stage holding hands with the cast.

I rapidly organised myself, rented an upright piano, bought a German grammar, and attended the innumerable weekly concerts. In my enthusiasm, I set myself high aims. First, I wanted to learn German well enough to be able to read Goethe and Schiller. This I never did. Second, to play at the piano the Strauss operas, an ambition which also remained unfulfilled. Third, to memorise Wagner's *Ring*, a task which I laboriously completed – eventually to find out that it was entirely unnecessary. I began to go through a vast musical literature of which I was ignorant. I attended Sunday services in churches where Masses by Mozart, Salieri, and Schubert were performed; I felt the magic spell of Bruckner's themes, although I found his works terribly long, and I could not understand why the second idea should be presented with such abruptness. But the nobility of his expression gave me tremendous joy and I was enthralled by his mysticism. The slow movement of the Seventh Symphony quite transported me; the Ninth Symphony gave me that feeling of majesty that one has facing a monolithic cathedral. Mahler was unknown to me, and in a few months I had the opportunity to listen to most of his symphonies. In my ignorance I failed at that time to see beyond the obvious vulgarity of his themes, though I recall being deeply moved by the *Kindertotenlieder* and *Des Knaben Wunderhorn*. Not anticipating what I discovered in his music thirty years later, I was disturbed by its lack of proportion, endless repetition, and the triviality of its expression. I did not understand, although I admired Mahler's skill in writing music, why his orchestration should bring in unexpected and unnecessary scurrility right in the middle of a phrase. I entirely failed to perceive his new outlook, his keen sense of colour, which had a great influence on modern music, although constantly remaining in the realm of tonality. Too occupied in assimilating the classics and the romantics, I missed the musical revolution on its way in Vienna.

The first snow had fallen, winter was setting in, three months had elapsed since my arrival, and I had already made several acquaintances. During a performance of *Falstaff*, I happened to be sitting next to a middle-aged man whom I will call Hans Kamper. He noticed my furtive glimpses at his score, and offered to share it with me. He had long greasy hair, thick glasses, and a pale flabby complexion. A fat protruding lower lip kept his mouth permanently open, exposing a set of unhealthy yellow teeth. He suggested I join him for a snack at a nearby café, where his wife was supposed to meet him after the performance. I accepted willingly. The lady was late, there was ample time for him to divest himself of his life history.

He was a composer, author of three operas, his musical streak originating from his Italian mother. Italy was the cradle of melody, German music was monstrous, Wagner the root of all evil. His unhappiness and misfortunes sprang from his father's Teutonic blood. His operas were never performed because of the scheming of a famous composer, whose reputation was undeserved and whose knowledge was overrated. He proved it. He sent his wife, posing as the mother of one of his students, to question the master on the boy's talent. She brought with her what was supposed to be the youngster's composition, having copied a Monteverdi motet note for note. The master, after careful examination, decided that the youth's musical aptitude was not outstanding. Would he put that in writing? The declaration was unequivocal: 'The lad's musical gift is inadequate: I do not advise his parents to embark on further expense to foster his musical education.'

The weapon for vengeance was at hand. Now he would harass his foe; he would persecute him out of existence. Thousands of photographic copies of the unfortunate remark printed next to the Monteverdi motet would tell the world of his rival's incompetence. His savings, devoted to the cause, were used to travel in foreign countries proclaiming his enemy's ignorance, distributing copies whenever the master was conducting a concert or one of his operas was being performed. He would sit in the balcony and in the interval drop hundreds of leaflets to disrupt the performance. He was twice arrested for causing trouble, but nothing would deter him from his mission. He journeyed from city to city pursuing his duty of destroying the man who could not feel the beauty of melodious music, the man incapable of differentiating a masterpiece from a youth's homework. His genius, his soul rich with music, could not flourish through the malice of an impostor!

Now he was poor, dejected, and compelled to give singing lessons in order to earn a living. He spoke monotonously, staring into the void, his facial muscles twitching every now and then. He hesitated for a while, then confessed that Mitzi for whom he was waiting was not his wife, but a kind person who pitied him and shared his lodgings. It was late at night, the coffee-house empty, the waiters upturning the chairs on the tables to clean the floor before closing. From the revolving door a woman in her early forties emerged hurriedly, making straight for us. She greeted me with indifference, then turned to speak to a waiter in a thick Viennese accent, while shaking a few snowflakes from her shabby fur coat. She was plump, common-looking and plain. Her simple nature was in striking contrast to her companion's bitter complexity. Puzzled, I accepted the offer to visit him three days later and listen to his music.

He lived in a big tenement house in a poor quarter of Vienna. It was almost a slum. To reach the third floor I had to make my way through a swarm of children playing marbles on the stairs. The composer himself answered the bell, while giggling girls peeped from the doors leading to the vestibule. The curiosity I aroused confirmed that my visit was expected, and that the singing lesson was being interrupted for my call. I was ceremoniously ushered into a large disorderly room, with a piano placed in the centre. There was no furniture in it beyond a bed used as a sofa and a chest surmounted with a painted bust of Verdi. The air was thick, and a variety of cheap female perfumes tempered by the pleasant scent of burning wood gave the place an atmosphere of sensuality. After a brief résumé of the libretto, my friend sat at the piano and started to play.

Singing teachers project musical dramas with convincing theatrical sense, suggesting with the voice, hinting at the action. The reading was powerful. At the end of the last act two grey bulging eyes stared at me inquiringly. My embarrassment left me silent, which he interpreted as approval. He got up, lit a cigar, and stretched contentedly on the sofa. I tried hard to find the expected word of praise, but I could not. In his self-complacency he had no doubts that I admired him. He was vain and devoid of any critical sense. I was confused: it was difficult to understand what kind of a man he was. He had contrived a libretto founded on silly coincidences, inspired by a cheap nineteenth-century novel. The music could have been a success if Puccini had not done it better thirty years before. He had neither individuality nor the intelligence to analyse himself. Self-indulgent and sentimental, he wrote sugary music to excite pity and admiration from the young girls of the singing class.

There was a young man there in his late twenties, a pupil of Schoenberg. I admired his gifts and his tenacity. He spoke to me about the twelve-tone system as the only language for future music, the system to express the tormented anguish of a modern world. Extremely progressive in his general outlook on art, and with remarkable literary knowledge, he struck a contrasting note in that carefree gathering. He stood a little apart from the group, observing the party with a slightly disdainful expression, a supercilious censor for anyone who ventured an ingenuous assertion. Only Mitzi with her naive charm was exempt from his scorn. He was an excellent pianist and I asked him to give me piano lessons twice a week. I visited him regularly at his lodgings, and after my lesson, as it was late in the day, we often dined at a nearby coffee-house and talked incessantly. He was a man of singular personality. Although his enormous knowledge of literature, philosophy and music gave a certain

76

sharpness to his way of conveying his thoughts, you soon had the feeling that for all his extensive studies he had acquired no assurance, only anxiety. Dismissive of my admiration for some inflated tone poems of Strauss, he would point out to me the beauty of the essential economy of Anton Webern's music, at the same time betraying a certain dissatisfaction with it. He also loved Mitzi desperately, and despised himself for loving such a plain woman Though filled with a rabid hatred of conventional society, he always wore a bowler hat and dressed in a black coat and striped trousers like a salesman in Fortnum & Mason. He loathed sentimentality, but I caught him with tears in his eyes when Furtwängler, conducting Brahms's Second Symphony, reached a moment of ecstasy at the end of the first movement, just after the horn solo. His peculiar personality made him unforgettable, and I grew fond of him. I was sorry when a year later he got a job as *Kapellmeister* in an opera house in the Rhineland and left Vienna. I expected he would find himself and make a great career, but he did not. I was told in later years he had married a woman for her intellect, but the union was a failure. He had abandoned music to teach philosophy and to be militant in an extreme leftist organisation. He died young. His body was found in a suburb of Prague, a bullet through his bowler hat.

It was at an Italian Embassy party in Vienna that I met Franz Schalk, director of the State Opera. The Italian Government had recently conferred on him a prestigious order, which explained his presence at such a strictly national gathering. His aura of celebrity and his own natural stiffness kept the guests at such a distance that to disguise his isolation he feigned an air of nonchalance, displaying a great show of interest in the paintings of the Metternich palace. Being myself without topics of conversation that could interest the wine or salami merchants who crowded the Italian colony in those days, I ventured to introduce myself to him to express my sincere admiration for his last stupendous performance of *Tristan and Isolde*. Pleased by my youthful enthusiasm, he invited me to sit with him, and inquired about my sojourn in Vienna. We sat on a comfortable sofa in a quiet smoking-room. His manner had the distant courtesy of a sovereign, his looks were those of a goat. He was thin, yellow and bony. A wrinkled neck emerged from a hard, turned-down collar, three or four sizes too large for him, and long emaciated hands protruded from starched cuffs. He showed a patronising interest in Italian musical life, and asked after his colleague 'the conductor of the Augusteo Orchestra, with a very small head and a violent temper', whose name he could not remember (Molinari). I told him how impressed I had been by the musical life in Vienna and by the young Wilhelm Furtwängler's concerts. He frowned and emitted a bleating sound. Furtwängler, he said emphatically, was only a 'talented amateur'. Obviously Furtwängler was not his favourite topic of conversation. I changed the subject.

Having read in the paper that in a few weeks' time he was to conduct the first performance in Vienna of *Oedipus Rex*, I asked his opinion of Stravinsky's music. Another bleat, this time louder than the last, accompanied a broad gesture of repugnance. Anxious to restore the former pleasant mood and to allay his evident annoyance, I unwarily inquired about Franco Alfano's new opera *Madonna Imperia,* coupled with Stravinsky on the bill. A long silence and a grimace of disgust kept me in suspense for a while. Then a long skinny hand patted my shoulder: 'Too French, young man, too French, *zu parfumiert.*' The contempt in his voice turned to veneration. 'Beethoven ... Brahms ... Bruckner ... !'

Judging it more advisable to turn the conversation to his performances of the classics, I mentioned how impressed I had been by his *Fidelio*, cautiously avoiding any praise of Beethoven's contribution. Our earlier cordiality was revived. We talked at length. Before leaving, he asked me if I would be interested in attending all the rehearsals at the Opera and in learning how a repertoire theatre is directed. My heart leapt. I waited anxiously for further news. A few days later I was summoned to his office and given an identity card that would get me past the well-guarded stage door, like any official member of the Opera House.

The State Opera was a meticulous bureaucracy. Its members had the demeanour of civil servants. Famous sopranos like Elizabeth Schumann, Lotte Lehmann and Wildbrunn arrived modestly like studious pupils to attend a morning rehearsal, having conscientiously learned their parts, so that the prompter had little to worry him. Idolised tenors like Schmedes, Slezak and Piccaver obeyed the theatre's strictest rules, rigidly controlled under Franz Schalk's supreme command. Every cog in the huge machinery worked smoothly, every detail planned in advance, nothing left to chance. The new productions were thoroughly rehearsed, the standard repertoire never. The result was interest and excitement for the *Neue Inszenierung*, dullness and routine for the rest. The *Generalmusikdirektor* conducted the important classical works and occasionally a modern one, leaving to the first conductor (Dr Heger), the second (Dr Alwin) and the third (Professor Reichenberger) the remaining repertoire in order of rank.

The Italian operas which occupied the major part of the bill were entrusted to Dr Alwin and Professor Reichenberger, whose conducting rendered the music unrecognisable. I had thought the Italians lacking in insight in their interpretation of German music, but the Germans, in those days, were considerably worse when they interpreted Verdi or Puccini. The orchestra, although far superior in quality to any Italian one, missed the vivacity, the bite and the clarity essential to Mediterranean music. A German orchestra's habit of playing after the conductor's beat, although producing an appropriately mellow sound for Wagner and Brahms, missed the explosive incisiveness necessary for Italian melodrama.

I recollect some inspired performances of Mozart's operas, the stirring *Elektra*s and *Salome*s with Strauss conducting. The first performance of Debussy's *Pelléas and Melisande* that I attended was well presented by the visiting Cologne Opera, with interesting avant-garde décor for those days, but the interpretation lacked the airy lightness of French music. During that winter *Das Wunder der Heliane* by Korngold was performed for the first time, and Krěnek's *Johnny Spielt Auf* amused the conservative Viennese. Schalk conducted (with no interest whatever) the long-awaited première of Stravinsky's *Oedipus Rex*, and paid scant attention to Alfano's *Madonna Imperia*. The composer, a mild-mannered Neapolitan, influenced by the French school, wrote pleasant music. Schalk, who looked down on Puccini, showed little love for Alfano's music, upsetting the composer to such a point that their relationship degenerated into raging hostility. The dissension between composer and conductor kept me busy carrying indirect messages to one and the other, employing tactful circumlocution to convey to Schalk that such a tempo was much too slow, or to inform Alfano that his rehearsal was cancelled in order to practise *Oedipus Rex* instead. Both works were a fiasco, and after the third performance were withdrawn from the repertoire. All this brought me closer to Schalk. Eventually he began inviting me home and allowed me into his rehearsals of the Philharmonic concerts, which was all valuable experience.

With plenty of time before me, and no distractions, I thought of trying my hand at composing. I believed I had a great deal to say, and I started a symphonic poem, venturing into a field more complex than any I had yet attempted. My previous essays, a short choral work on a poem by d'Annunzio, and a few songs for voice and orchestra written while at the Conservatory in Florence, denoted sensibility but an embarrassing lack of originality. Now, with a particular idea having been tormenting my mind for months, I thought it was about time to put it down on paper. I began to work. For weeks I developed my theme; I gave it unity and shape, I discarded the original fancy of three movements. I lessened the length, made it in one mould, with an introduction, a climax and an end. I was ingenuously happy with the piece and I set about orchestrating it. There is something deeply satisfying about assigning parts to various orchestral groups, blending the colours, giving a vivid brush-stroke to a culminating point, and finally seeing something one had in mind transformed into reality.

Three months later it was finished. I thought it was clever, full of amusing details, with elegant effects showing a gift for colour, but nothing more. I did not dare to seek counsel from Schalk, since the music was much too impressionistic for his taste, nor from my piano teacher whose preference was for Webern and Schoenberg rather than for Debussy and Ravel. Eventually I tired of the piece, put it away in a drawer and forgot about it.

My father came to visit me in mid-winter. He lodged in a hotel on the Kärtnerstrasse and I enjoyed introducing him to the city – he did not speak a word of German. We met as two friends meet; we invited each other to meals; I took him to the Opera (*Marriage of Figaro*), which he liked immensely, and to a Phil-harmonic concert (Kleiber conducting Beethoven's Seventh) of which he said he rather fancied the 'tic-tic-tic' of the strings in the second movement. (I surmised it was the *fugato* section.) We went to several plays; even though ignorant of the language, he loved the fine acting. He visited all the museums, and he was attracted by a Titian in the National Gallery, rather similar to a sombre painting he had hanging in a neglected room of our country place. He undertook painstaking researches, eventually establishing that Titian had painted three canvases on the same subject. One was in Vienna, the second was destroyed by a fire in Venice, and the third was lost. It was a few months later that, intrigued by this, he began to clean the canvas of the accumula-tion of centuries-old dust and mildew. As if by magic, at each

MF's father, c.1903.

sweep of the sponge ravishing colours came to light. With suppressed excitement he uncovered more and more, until on the turban of a figure the 'three flowers on a branch' emerged, a signature sometimes used by Titian. My grandfather had bought the picture for only a few liras in Leghorn in a junk shop, and it now adorns a museum somewhere in the United States.

I was very sorry to see my father leave Vienna, as we had grown closer during his stay there. He had been very tactful in avoiding questions as to my studies and plans for the future, but while walking together on the platform of the Südbahnhof, waiting for the train to leave, he spoke of 'life as a long and arduous uphill road to be conquered with hard work and integrity'.

From Vienna I went to Paris. A letter of introduction from my father to a friend from his days at Geneva University brought me into contact with an ultra-conservative literary group; through a friend in Vienna I became acquainted with a Bohemian set of painters; and through an aunt I was introduced into the stuffy French aristocracy. I found myself living in three different groups which had no connection with one another. I kept my activities jealously concealed from set to set, independently enjoying three different facets of Parisian life.

Father's friend, Pierre Paul Plan, lived in a narrow street not far from the Comédie Française, in a building that two centuries ago had been occupied by people of means. It was a substantial house with an impressive entrance, now decayed through climatic inclemency and neglect. He was a cynic, and led a solitary life. When a convulsive shaking of a bell, set into motion from the street by a primitive system of linking wires, warned of a visitor, he gave a mistrustful look between the uneven battens of the rotting shutters to verify the identity of the caller. In the spacious entrance hundreds of books, complimentary copies sent by editors, lay in disorderly fashion over tables and chairs and on the floor. Many, still new, had the unbroken coloured band advertising the prize they had won. He was a classicist, and had little admiration for contemporary literature. Once, when I was caught glancing at a book by Cocteau – *Les Mariés de la Tour Eiffel* – he sarcastically rebuked me: 'This is not literature, this is rubbish.'

His study, by contrast, was a model of tidiness: books neatly stacked on shelves, beautiful editions of the complete works of Racine, Molière, Voltaire and so on adorning his bookcases. The room, probably once the ballroom, was large. The ceiling was decorated with Egyptian frescoes from the Napoleonic period. A long refectory table occupying the centre of the room was covered with neatly gathered manuscripts fastened with ribbons and labelled with tags. Apart from the table, there was a desk of an indefinite style, a standard lamp, a chair, a springless greasy sofa and a threadbare rug. Three windows down to the floor made the room cold.

Originally from Geneva, Plan had moved with his sister to Paris at the end of the last century. Since her death twenty-five years previously, he had led a solitary life in the same large house they had first occupied in 1897. A grumpy charwoman, toothless and dishevelled, wrapped in a shawl and dragging an old pair of grey slippers, moved aimlessly around the house mumbling who knows what kinds of insults about the rare visitor. She took superficial care of the cleaning, cooked one meal, and occasionally mended his socks. The pattern of his life was unconventional. He got up at half-past five in the afternoon, sitting down to work until nine in the evening. He then walked to a nearby restaurant for a meal before going to his job as literary critic of the *Journal des Débats*. At four in the morning he returned home to eat a frugal supper left on the stove by the daily. He sat at his desk until the first rays of the sun filtered through the shutters, working on J. J. Rousseau's correspondence – a huge task which occupied the greater part of his life. This nocturnal existence made his complexion ivory-coloured; the two dark eyes burned with intensity deep in their sockets. He

84

was tall and thin, his voice was rich and musical. He spoke beautiful French, with an old-fashioned classicism, elegantly phrased. It was hard to guess his age: he might not have been more than sixty, but his bent body and the pallor of his face made him appear much older.

I regularly visited him twice a week, fascinated by his personality and proud to be with such a scholar. He had no practical sense and no interest in modern inventions (he once told me that he had never been to the cinema). His life was dedicated to literature, and he thought that Voltaire was the last French writer. The modern writers ... 'des fumistes'. He loved music, but only Rameau and Mozart really satisfied him. The first, for his classical eloquence, without the pomposity and bloatedness of Gluck; the second, for his absolute perfection. We often walked from his house to the nearby restaurant he had patronised for twenty years and where a corner table was reserved for him. After meals I accompanied him to the newspaper office for his nightly work. I always tried to get him to speak of literature, and of his friendships with Anatole France and Paul Verlaine. He was somewhat scholastic in his conversation, although his sense of humour, his sharp turn of phrase and an occasional sarcastic glance from the corner of his eyes made him amusing. He thought the modern writers deficient in the use of epithets, having little regard for the significance of the phrase, wanting in grammar and poetic power. With his prodigious memory he could cite Molière's or Voltaire's use of adjectives, and their skill in finding appropriate expressions. Platitudes or weaknesses in style brought on a passionate diatribe of invective. His wealth of imagery amounted to genius. I often purposely quoted expressions from books just published in order to provoke his reaction. It was a fruitful lesson in French literature.

Paris at that time had a fascination which I think has vanished today. Ladies of the aristocracy and the *haute bourgeoisie* opened their doors to writers, painters and musicians: some had a day every week for their friends to drop in – Thursdays at Marie Louise Bousquet, Sundays at the Godebskis, with Gide, Ravel, Roussel, Misia Sert, Jacques de Lacretelle and Raynaldo Hahn. It was a world of elegant dinner parties, Cocteau's mimicry, Rubinstein's storytelling, gossip, intrigues, all seasoned with caustic French wit. Amused by the life, I spent my time going from one party to another. I would not say that those two years in Paris provided me with the most valuable experience, but I had the opportunity of witnessing a period that marked the end of a great era and the adventurous search for new horizons. Stravinsky had previously broken the rules with *Le Sacre du Printemps* and Picasso was already launched into cubism. Diaghilev acted as a catalyst for artistic talent; Cocteau, pontiff of witchery and dilettantism, played with his followers like puppets. There was a stimulating feeling of creativity. I was a mere spectator and benefited from it. I did nothing productive, but I do not regret any time lost. I enjoyed these characters, and especially their *joie de vivre*.

All Paris knew the story of the incident which took pace when the seventeen-year-old Igor Markevitch, leaving La Salle Pleyel after the successful première of one of his early compositions, ran into Sulima Stravinsky, the composer's son. After the requisite congratulations, Sulima said, 'But it must be an embarrassment being called Igor.' The instant retort was 'Not nearly as much as being called Stravinsky.'

The charm of Paris in the late Twenties was created by a large number of people who expanded in their daily lives more than in their works. Artur Rubinstein, for instance, although in those days a brilliant virtuoso, was more of a celebrity for his immense vitality, his wit as a storyteller, his attraction for women, and his magnetic charm, than for his *pianisme*. His technique was occasionally at fault for lack of study. It happened once that, having to practise for a future concert, he instructed his butler, Jean, not to bother him with lady admirers' telephone calls. He was playing the *Fire Dance* of de Falla, when the telephone rang. Jean picked up the receiver and a female voice asked for the *Maître*. 'No, madame, Mr Rubinstein is not at home.'

'But I can hear him playing the piano.'

'Oh no, madame, it is I who am dusting the keyboard.'

Quoting Maurice Sachs (one of the young men of that time who fulfilled his early promise), 'When Rubinstein entered a salon and kissed a lady's hand, the rape of Europa took place all over again.'

Among the painters during my time in Paris, Pavel Tchelichew was the most captivating and the most interesting personality of all. A thin, nervous man in his thirties, smartly dressed, with squinting eyes and a vivacious wit, he never wasted any time with the Bohemians at the Dôme or the Coupole. He led an organised life, sharing his house with Allen Tanner, an American pianist. He painted, at that time, in sombre colours, with greyish-green figures whose faces wore tormented expressions. There was a deep melancholy in his character, and one sensed his feverish struggle in search of the sublime. As he lived in the Boulevard Montparnasse, only a few houses away from my lodgings, I often stopped at his studio for a chat. His attractive personality was a mixture of conflicting elements. He was a mystic, a devout believer, hypersensitive, superstitious, egotistic, moody, pagan, influenced by astrology, and above all, a great charmer.

Alexander Steinert was an American amateur pianist and composer. His family, originally from Germany, emigrated to the United States a few generations ago. His father started a music store in Boston and made a conspicuous fortune; eventually his business had such prestige that the Steinway piano firm appointed him their representative in New England. Young Alec grew up in a musical world. Most of the celebrated pianists, being Steinway artists, were guests of his parents every time they played in Boston. His father kept up the traditional generous hospitality of the Steinway family in New York and Alec met all the musical celebrities. Koussewitzky once performed a tone poem of his called *Leggenda Sinfonica*.

In the late Twenties he married a pretty American girl and they went to live in Paris. They bought a lovely house in rue Raynouard, where Balzac wrote most of his books – you could still see the trapdoor through which he used to escape when the creditors were after him. The drawing-room was large, with a circular gallery that led to the first floor. Alec immediately installed two Steinway grands in the centre of the room and his *musicales* were almost nightly events that lasted until the early hours.

One night, in spite of the presence of some highly distinguished celebrities, including Furtwängler, the hostess, whose musicality did not match her beauty, appeared in the gallery in her nightgown – her hair dishevelled like a Fury's – and made such a scene about the noise that everybody left, one by one, like beaten dogs. Not the ideally supportive partner for someone of Alec's tastes, eventually she left him and married a sea captain.

I first met Nathan Milstein at one of these parties. The American season was over and the virtuosi, returning to Europe, gathered in Paris for the spring. Koussewitzky, Stokowski, Fritz Kreisler and the three young Russians, Horowitz, Milstein and Piatigorsky were frequent visitors at the Steinerts. I have known Milstein now for over sixty years and we have played together on innumerable occasions. I admire his straightforwardness and simplicity

The first time Horowitz and I played together was in Warsaw in 1932, and after that we played many times in the United States. I used to see him often when I lived there. He used to come to spend long weekends with us on the farm in Connecticut, sometimes settled at the piano until three or four in the

MF and Nathan Milstein rehearsing, 1950.

morning. A special sense of humour and a streak of naivety combined to make him a most endearing companion, though in common with many artists he appeared on occasion to believe that the world existed for him alone. There was, for example, a tragi-comic incident after our first concert in Warsaw. He had played Rachmaninov's Third Concerto with such enormous success that the whole city was buzzing. The next day we both left for the station to catch the train to Berlin. We were looking out of the window of the sleeper, waiting for departure, when a pair of newlyweds arrived, she still in her wedding gown, he in a

Vladimir Horowitz sunning himself, Connecticut, 1948.

morning coat, followed by a crowd of relations and friends carrying bouquets of flowers and boxes of sweets. Suddenly some members of the party recognised Horowitz and the whole throng abandoned the honeymooners and rushed towards our sleeping-car, festooning him with flowers and chocolates. As the train drew out Horowitz was acknowledging his admirers' applause with a royal gesture, while the bridal couple watched disconsolately from their compartment. I can still see the girl's expression as Horowitz stole her show. He took it all for granted, probably without even an inkling of what he was doing to her.

Moody and capricious in his private life, he is logical and disciplined when it comes to music. His conception of a work is thought out to such a point that his interpretations, sustained by an immaculate technical clarity, are wholly convincing, his liberties in performance always right. There is not much more that one can say about him. He is a genius.

In the past few years we have seen each other often in London when he has come for a concert engagement on his way to Germany, France, Japan or Italy. Our friendship is still the same. Once he telephoned me to ask me if I still liked music. I said yes. 'Come to the Connaught, I want to play two Scarlatti sonatas for you.' I arrived at noon and stayed until six in the evening. He played me the whole programme for his concert in the Festival Hall.

Now he does not want to travel. We occasionally talk on the telephone, but his wife Wanda, the dear friend of my youth, frequently comes to London and keeps our friendship very much alive.

An elderly couple whom I met through Hélène Casella, the composer's first wife, often invited me to their house. They lived the other side of Paris – 22 rue d'Athène, a noisy street in a commercial district. I knew their name long before I was to meet them: when I was a young boy the piece of music that used to move me to tears was Ravel's *Sonatine*, dedicated to Ida and Cipa Godebski. Another work by Ravel (which, when I was a child, in one of my morbid moods I wanted to be played at my funeral) was 'Le Jardin Féerique' from *Ma Mère l'Oye*, also dedicated to the Godebskis' two children, Mimi and Jean. For years I had been puzzled by the name Godebski. I often wondered who they were, and why Ravel had dedicated the five *Pièces Enfantines* to them.

The Godebskis, originally Polish, had the warmth and the exuberance of the Slavs, mellowed by a long sojourn in France. Their apartment was often a meeting place for painters and musicians; Ravel frequently stopped for a visit at rue d'Athène before catching the train back to his suburban house. At the time of our meeting, the Godebskis, Mimi and Jean, were no longer the two children of *Mother Goose*. The first was a married woman of great beauty, the second a university student. I had an affectionate feeling for Ida and Cipa, for their exquisite hospitality, and still have a vivid memory of meeting Maurice Ravel for the first time at their house.

I had been invited one afternoon for a cup of tea when this thin little man, with grey hair, reddish complexion and sharp pointed nose entered the room. My veneration for his music was such that his presence made me shy and somewhat confused. He addressed a few polite words to me, which I don't think I answered, and turned to talk to our hostess. He differed greatly from the man I had imagined. I expected him to be more of a poet, with dreamy eyes and charm. Instead I found him rather frigid, with a chip on his shoulder, a sarcastic sense of humour, mordant wit, but no conceit. From his extraordinary compositions for the piano I supposed he would have beautiful hands, but his hands in fact were large and coarse, his fingers chubby, the tips almost square.

Many years later, Zino Francescatti told me a story about Ravel's clumsy technique. They were both touring England, Ravel accompanying *Tzigane* at the piano. His plump fingers had serious trouble playing the difficult piano part. This awkwardness caused Ravel such anxiety that he could not thoroughly concentrate on what Francescatti was playing. Notwithstanding, at the end of each performance he invariably declared: 'Zino, at a certain spot you always play a wrong note.' Francescatti, concerned by this, asked the composer where the offending note could be. They both examined the score, but Ravel was unable to find it. 'I will let you know after the next performance.' Concert after concert, the same assertion from Ravel, the same concern from Francescatti; yet the wrong note was never discovered.

Many months later, while Francescatti was resting during the summer in his house in Marseilles, his mother, an excellent violinist, asked him to play *Tzigane*. All of a sudden, in the middle of a piece, she cried: 'But Zino . . . you played a wrong note!'

'But where, Mother?'

'Right here,' she replied, pointing at a spot in the score. The mystery was solved.

After that first meeting I saw Ravel now and then at parties. It was about a year later that Madame Casella arranged that I should ask his advice and opinion as to my aptitude as a composer. A date was settled for our meeting and I left that morning for his home on the outskirts of Paris, with the 'Poem for Orchestra' which I had composed two years previously in Vienna. I was cordially received. I remember nothing of the short preliminary conversation we had before he examined my score. He then sat down at the piano, placing the music on a board near the keys, in such a way that by spinning on the revolving stool he could comfortably play some passages on the instrument. The sepulchral silence was occasionally interrupted by the turning of the pages. After a primary analysis he returned once more for a second reading to the beginning of the piece – this time frequently interrupting himself to congratulate me on my keen and sensitive approach to the conception of orchestral sound, on my technical ability, on my knowledge in balancing the sonority of the wind section versus the strings, on my skilled treatment of a large group of percussionists. It was after a long silence that he looked me straight in the eyes. I was calmly awaiting the verdict. 'Mon cher jeune homme,' he said, 'tout ça est très bien, mais . . . c'est du Ravel!' If that was the best that could be said about my originality, perhaps I was better off conducting other people's music.

In 1932 Arturo Toscanini came on a tour of Europe with the New York Philharmonic Orchestra. After four spectacular concerts in London, two in the Queen's Hall and two at the Albert Hall, his next stop was Paris.

The afternoon of the concert I had tea with Madame Casella at her flat, and she told me that she had met Ravel in the street that morning dressed in his usual light grey suit, on his way home. She had asked if he was going to the concert that evening. 'No,' he had answered curtly, 'I haven't been invited to hear *le grand virtuoso*.' Madame Casella, upset by the reply, offered him a ticket she had been keeping for a friend.

That night I saw both of them at the Théâtre de l'Opéra sitting in the stalls three rows in front of me. The hall was packed with a glittering audience, who gave the concert a rapturous reception. Ravel's *Bolero,* the final piece, kept them transfixed – from the almost inaudible *pianissimo* of the snare-drum at the beginning to the luminous climax of the E major chords at the end. As the masterly controlled crescendo died away, there was a frenzy of applause, everyone on their feet, shouting, waving programmes, handbags, even furs.

Toscanini, on being told by his concert master, Scipione Guidi, of Ravel's presence in the hall, repeatedly beckoned the composer to share his triumph. The audience awaited for Ravel to get up and acknowledge the applause. Ravel refused. Still dressed in his grey suit, he sat unmoved during the fifteen-minute ovation.

I was present in the artists' room after the concert when he shook hands with Toscanini. 'Deux fois trop vite,' he said coldly, 'deux fois trop vite.' Then he turned away and left the room.

Although I had read a great deal on conducting technique, I had my doubts about just how useful all the books would be when one actually came to conduct an orchestra. The graphic designs that a baton should follow (in Scherchen's book *Über des Dirigieren*) I found elementary and useless, because a conductor's movements are subject to his own individuality and to his personal interpretation of how a phrase should be shaped. I finally concluded that a conductor must attain his skill by conducting a real orchestra, not an imaginary one; and as, alas, one cannot have an orchestra at one's disposal to practise with, one has to acquire one's experience at the expense of the public.

I knew that a ballet company was about to be formed in Paris around the famous name of Antonia Mercé, 'La Argentina', a Spaniard born in Buenos Aires who made classical arrangements of Spanish dances. Large groups of dancers were being engaged, and there was much excitement about the opening, which was to take place at the Opéra Comique. There was then to be a month

Mme Argentina.

on tour, followed by a long series of performances at the Théâtre Marigny in Paris.

I called on a friend, the Cuban pianist-composer, Joaquin Nin, who had some connection with the organisers, and explained my predicament. I had little hope, as I had really nothing to offer. I simply wanted the chance of facing a professional orchestra. He put me in touch with the manager of the Spanish ballet company and a few days later I was asked for an interview. Somehow I summoned up the courage to climb the stairs to the third-floor office. At each step I felt that I was being dragged down by a mysterious force on my left telling me to run away while there was still time. On my right a voice was whispering 'Don't be a coward; if you don't go up you will be lost for ever.'

I found myself perspiring, sitting on a leather armchair in front of a desk. A small man in a brown suit sat on the other side and scarcely looked at me. He was blond, with a round head, and spoke with a soft monotonous voice with a thick Russian accent. His eyes were blue, underhung by two large brown circles. To my considerable relief he did not ask me what I had to offer, but told me in a dull voice that the principal conductor was Monsieur G. L. of the Opéra Comique and that he was to conduct all the performances unless something unexpected happened. I would be assistant conductor and as such had to know the repertoire and be ready for any eventuality. My salary would be 150 francs daily. Needless to say I accepted.

The success was enormous: the *tout Paris* was flocking to see the 'Argentina', the press was enthusiastic, and I sat backstage awaiting the eventuality.

A few days later, thanks to the famous Italian tenor Lauri Volpi, I had my chance. We were on tour performing at the Casino de Vichy when Monsieur G. L. went to see the sad little manager to inform him that the celebrated tenor refused to sing in Paris unless he, Monsieur G. L., conducted, since he alone knew all the liberties the tenor took when singing Puccini. He demanded a gigantic sum if he were to remain with the company.

The soft-spoken manager said 'No.' Half an hour later I received a call at my hotel: 'Tonight you conduct.'

I will say little of my first experience in conducting. The orchestra was already rehearsed by the principal conductor, and I only had to step into the pit occasionally to carry on with the agreed interpretation. Furthermore, with a ballet on stage I had to keep a set rhythm so as not to upset the steps of the dancers. The music we played was beautiful (Granados, de Falla, Albeniz). One night, many performances later, I forgot after the introduction to ring the bell warning the stage-hand to raise the curtain. I was happily going on with my music when I noticed a worried expression on the faces of some of the orchestra. It was too late. When the curtain went up, my oversight had ruined La Argentina's entrance of which she was so proud. Tears, apologies followed, but I fear I was never forgiven. The experience was very salutary.

I discovered that I was self-conscious and stiff and therefore unable to let the musical discourse flow as smoothly as I wanted. I realised that the profession I was entering involved not only complete knowledge of the score, but the development of my individual technique in order to impart my concepts to an orchestra. Moreover, an orchestra was an instrument made up of rational beings, reacting to one's precision of thought, ability to project, and psychological approach. I believe I learned a great deal through the many rehearsals I had attended, but although it had not been a waste of time (if only for the pleasure of listening to some beautiful music), it had not been too fruitful either, because each conductor has his own ascendancy and his own inimitable way of moulding a performance.

After my first engagement Alfredo Casella introduced me to a group promoting solely contemporary music, as the result of which I conducted a concert of modern Italian composers. From then on I seized every opportunity of confronting an orchestra. But my stock-in-trade was limited and my repertoire extended to only two or three programmes. Although I had a natural

THÉATRE MARIGNY

DIRECTION : LÉON VOLTERRA

LES REPRÉSENTATIONS DE MADAME

ARGENTINA

AVEC SA TROUPE DE BALLETS ESPAGNOLS

L'orchestre sera dirigé par Monsieur Georges LAUWERYNS
Deuxième Chef d'Orchestre : Monsieur M. FRECCIA

Juillet 1929   DIX FRANCS

'Deuxième Chef d'Orchestre.'

clear beat, I did not yet have the emotional control of a score's dramatic sections; I found myself involved in too many climaxes, at the same time missing their culminating moments through unbalanced sonorities, and in wasting too much energy in exciting emotions unnecessarily. The discovery of my limitations forced me to find a remedy. I had to get my experience somewhere other than Paris. I had the feeling that I had spent my last two years at a world fair, in a city of intellectual acrobats, a showcase for artists and writers illuminated by glittering social display. I missed real music, and I returned to Vienna.

An unexpected invitation to conduct a concert with the Wiener Sinphoniker brought me into contact with the Austrian musical world. It was a moderate success, but my totally unknown name was noticed by a Hungarian gentleman who found himself by chance at the concert. His name was Gustav Barczy. He owned the Budapest music publishing house Rószasavölgyi and a concert agency. He had just organised a new orchestra, the Budapest Symphony, from selected students from the Conservatory. The quality of the strings was excellent as most of the violinists were pupils of the celebrated Erno Hubay.

Mr Barczy needed a young conductor to grow with the orchestra and I was asked to conduct a concert as a test. Aladár Toth, the famous critic of the *Pesti Naplo,* reviewed the concert with enthusiasm, and Mr Barczy, pleased with my success, offered me more concerts and the post of permanent conductor for the following season. He had booked as guest conductors such illustrious names as Richard Strauss, Weintgartner, Klemperer, Erich Kleiber and Bruno Walter.

My stay in Budapest was most stimulating. I struck up a great friendship with Sergio Failoni, the already well-known Italian conductor of the Budapest Opera. His talent was exceptional and his personality highly amusing. I often met, too, Zoltan Kodaly, Leo Weiner and Béla Bartók, and had the honour to

MF conducting the Budapest Symphony Orchestra, 1934.

conduct on 24 January 1932 the first performance of Bartók's *Rumanian Dances*, a piece written originally for piano. Bartók was fascinated by the folklore of Transylvania, and the brilliant orchestration of the piece gave ample opportunity to the clarinettists to show their virtuosity. At one rehearsal I asked Bartók to come on stage and explain how the gypsies would phrase the melody. He did so, and sung the phrase to the clarinets in the gypsy idiom. He was a quiet, unassuming man, but could be very warm and cordial. Although in America I had news of him through our mutual friend Giorgy Sandor, the last time I saw him was in Carnegie Hall in the interval of a concert. He died shortly after.

When the war was over I received several messages from Aladár Toth through Alexander Sved, the baritone, asking me to return to Budapest, but at that time I thought I could not go back to the city I had loved so much. Toth had been named Director of the Budapest Opera and had married Annie Fischer. The last time I heard from him was in 1964 when she played with me in Berlin.

I went back to conduct in Budapest in 1969. Toth, Weiner, Failoni, Bartók and Kodaly were all gone ... the city had changed but I had great pleasure when I recognised in the leader of the Hungarian State Orchestra the blond man who sat in the second violin section of the Budapest Symphony Orchestra before the war.

In 1934, at the end of the second year of my engagement in Budapest, I conducted the orchestra on a tour of ten concerts in Italy, including one in Rome where the Italian and Spanish Royal Families and Benito Mussolini were present. Then a message arrived. It was curt and concise: I was expected the following day at 11 a.m. by the 'Capo del Governo' at Palazzo Venezia. Needless to say, I was there ten minutes before my appointment. I sat on a straight-backed chair in a spacious room where a Mongolian-looking gentleman, apparently also awaiting his audience, was showing distinct signs of nerves.

At exactly eleven o'clock two officers in Fascist uniforms informed me that I would be received by the Duce in a few moments. They then escorted me into the salon which he used as his study. This historic room was of epic length; it held no furniture except for a refectory table with one large chair at the far side facing two small ones for visitors.

The journey seemed interminable. To relieve one's embarrassment while covering the distance to the other end of the room, the Duce kept himself busy sorting a few papers that were scattered over the table. It was only when I was within a few feet of him that he raised his head, stood up, walked around the table and asked me to sit down on one of the two chairs facing him. He immediately started to talk about my concert the previous evening; he had been most impressed by the string section and by the excellence of the ensemble with which I had been touring Italy. He told me that he himself had studied the violin, and he admired the precision of the violins in Beethoven's Seventh Symphony in particular. Our conversation was interrupted just as we had reached the *fugato* of the second movement. The two officers re-entered the room, opened the balcony windows and stood aside, waiting for the Duce. Mussolini went out onto the balcony, to be greeted by a storm of applause, with people shouting and waving flags. It was a tremendous explosion of enthusiasm. He addressed the crowd for about twenty minutes, with intense passion. At the end of the harangue he stepped back into the room, walked straight up to me and resumed the conversation at the exact point where we had left off. This power of concentration impressed me tremendously. I was very struck by his voice, by his penetrating eyes, by his articulateness and by an unexpected warmth.

He told me that I should remain in Italy to develop my artistic activities, and suggested that I should talk to his son-in-law, Galeazzo Ciano (at that time Minister of the Cultura Popolare). I felt that this venture would involve me with the political setup in Italy, so I left it well alone.

That summer I decided to spend a month on a Mediterranean island, just to enjoy a warm, primitive, pagan existence. I rented a room in a house on a reef; it belonged to the owner of a restaurant, who fed his customers on a platform consisting of a few planks built on piles extending over the sea. My accommodation was very simple: an iron bed, a basin and a chair. At the back of the house, a pail of water provided my daily shower. Early each morning I set out in a sculler with a frugal luncheon and returned at sunset after a day spent investigating the inlets and grottoes which surrounded the island.

It was in one of these creeks that I encountered a young girl who swam from the other side of the bay when the sea was not too rough. I was eating my usual sandwich in a cove when she came ashore. She looked beautiful. Her long wet hair clung to her, the drops of water on her skin iridescent in the sun. I offered her half of a sandwich I had brought with me, she accepted it, and we became friends. She returned daily to the same place.

Late one hot evening, I decided to walk up to the village to buy a newspaper as I had not read anything of what had happened to the world in more than two weeks. At the bar of a hotel, where I stopped for a whisky and soda before returning home, I found an old friend whom I had not seen for a year. He had married in the meantime, and he introduced me to his wife. We talked for about an hour. I then resumed my walk to the beach through the usual short cut. The night was dark, and I could hardly see the narrow footpath leading to my lodgings. I was assaulted by two men.

The scuffle did not last long, darkness was in my favour and I think that the two aggressors inflicted on each other most of the blows that were meant for me. But the incident shocked the inhabitants of the island who were astonished that two gentlemen of a distinguished family, as it turned out, should behave in such a disgraceful manner. Eventually we discovered that a powerful Fascist industrialist, a keen admirer of the young swimmer, had instigated the attack by the two brothers. So two days later my seconds presented the older of the two assailants with a formal challenge to a duel.

In the course of the next three days several meetings took place between the two seconds from both sides. The incident had been violent and the terms demanded by my supporters were harsh. Pistols were discarded and swords were chosen as being more lethal than sabres. This meant that I was at a disadvantage. My opponent was a cavalry officer, and fencing was compulsory in the Italian army; I had taken fencing lessons only as a young boy.

The duel was scheduled for a week later to give me time to get into practice. Having heard that there was a famous swordsman in Naples who sounded just what I needed, I immediately contacted him at his school. He received me in a large hall, the walls covered with photographs of his triumphs. Silver cups and trophies filled a showcase. He was dressed in the uniform of a fencing master, all in white, with a quilted jacket buttoned on his left shoulder. If his looks were not friendly – a haughty face, jaw covered by a grizzled beard – his manners were civil and he showed concern for my predicament. He wanted to know the age, height and build of my opponent and anything else I knew about him. Then he brusquely told me to return the next day for a two-hour training session in the morning and another in the afternoon.

The drilling was hard. He did not allow me to wear a visor so that I would get used to seeing the tip of my adversary's sword a few inches from my eyes when the two hand-guards met. For a week I lived with the noise of our stamping feet on the wooden platform and the clashing of the swords. He taught me not to charge as I was not as experienced as my adversary, but to maintain teasing tactics of defence that would tempt him to attack and eventually to lose control, thus leaving an opening for my thrust.

My brother came from Florence to keep me company. He helped me prepare my gear: we cut the right sleeve off a shirt, took away all the buttons, and chose a belt not exceeding the width prescribed by the rules. At five in the morning I was fetched by my seconds to go to the appointed place.

The sun was rising when we reached the lonely spot; an opalescent vapour hung low over the ground. My car and what I took to be my opponent's car stopped some distance away, while a third car pulled up at the place where we were to fight. Four gentlemen got out of it. Two of them opened a collapsible table and deposited on top of it the suitcase they had brought with them. The others inspected the ground meticulously, taking measurements with great precision. They were all formally dressed.

I was still waiting in my car, intrigued by the developments, when a gentleman not known to me took a long narrow package wrapped in green felt out of the boot of his vehicle. It contained the swords. Then, accompanied by my two seconds, I was escorted to the site where the engagement had to be fought. The doctor and the surgeon had neatly placed some surgical instruments, medical bottles and bandages on one side of the table; on the other, there were three swords, one for each adversary, the third for the *direttore del combattimento*.

From then on everything moved fast. After the surgeon had sterilised the blades, the *direttore* allotted a weapon to each contestant, and ordered us to take our places. The brief ritual salute was followed by numerous assaults; my opponent, trying to break through my guard, got so excited that his sword fell from his hand. The *direttore* interrupted us for a further sterilisation of the blade. We then resumed the fight. He became more and more confident, constantly on the attack. Then, in a moment of uncontrolled aggression, he suddenly left a gap open for my thrust. My sword pierced his right arm, a few inches below the shoulder.

The *direttore* stopped the duel. While my opponent was taken aside for medical treatment, I was asked by my seconds to wait on the spot. It was after a good fifteen minutes that we were informed that he could not continue the fight, and that he had admitted defeat.

My return to the island was enthusiastically received. The powerful Fascist, instigator of the whole drama, who had announced that I would never come back, had left, disappointed, for Rome. A leading nobleman from Naples and his wife gave a dinner party for me as a final seal of approval. It was the end of an era when chivalry and the code of honour still had a meaning. More important, I still had a life.

Two months later I encountered in Paris, by chance, a young French couple whom I had met on the island. We talked once more about the dramatic incident. He told me, 'You were a fool to stir trouble with a young unmarried girl. My wife would have loved to go out with you.' I issued no challenge.

After my father's death I decided to go to New York. In the autumn of 1937, a few months after my arrival, I was asked by the New York Philharmonic Orchestra to conduct a series of

Moritz Rosenthal (a pupil of Liszt) and MF at rehearsal of New York Philharmonic, Lewisohn Stadium, 1938.

concerts at the Lewisohn Stadium the following year. The news surprised me, as I had never dreamed of getting such an opportunity in so short a time. Apparently Mrs Guggenheimer, Chairman of the Board, in the course of a conversation with Toscanini about musical life in Italy, had asked the Maestro if there were any up and coming young conductors. Toscanini mentioned me as a young man who was doing well in Europe and who had conducted recently at La Scala with success. His words started the ball rolling.

I returned to Italy for appearances with the Santa Cecilia Orchestra in Rome, and sailed back in the spring of 1938 for my début in New York. Walter Damrosch, the dean of American conductors, had the traditional honour of leading the first night of the season. I followed with a long series of concerts immediately after. My success was instantaneous and quite unexpected. My name, hitherto completely unknown in America, gained a certain éclat in the musical world right after the first rehearsal. The hard-boiled New York Philharmonic Orchestra, after the first run-through of Ravel's *Daphnis and Chloe* Second Suite, showed such enthusiasm and cooperation that my fortunes were made in the weeks to come. My concerts received public acclaim and the most important papers praised my performances almost unanimously. As José Iturbi had to cancel his concerts that season with the New York Philharmonic at the Lewisohn Stadium, I was asked to take over his commitments.

I was in Rome. I had been rehearsing all afternoon and, coming back to my hotel, I was looking forward to a hot bath, a drink, a meal, and a peaceful evening in which to prepare for the following day's rehearsal. I was getting out of the bath when the telephone rang. I answered it in the sitting-room, dripping wet. It was the hall porter to tell me there was a Mr Allen downstairs who wanted very much to see me. I knew no one of that name in Rome and thought it must be a mistake. No, said the porter, the gentleman knew me well. I told him to ask my visitor to come up to my suite, but first give me time to dress.

When I opened the door I recognised in 'Mr Allen' Leopold Stokowski. He was dressed in his usual eccentric way and his accent was more affected than ever. He seized my hands, both of them, and shook them warmly. I asked him to come in and have a drink – I could offer him whisky, gin, vodka or sherry. He wanted raspberry syrup. I managed to get some sent up from the bar.

He told me he had seen my name on the posters in the street and had succeeded in finding out the name of the hotel in which I was staying through the Accademia di Santa Cecilia. He was extremely cordial; he inquired about the orchestra (pronouncing it with the accent on the 'e') and asked if I still stayed at the Sulgrave Hotel in New York (pronouncing Sulgrave as if it were a French name). He told me how much he loved Italy, a country where things were still made by hand – even the roadworks were patched up manually, not like in America with those 'horrible bulldozers'. I was listening to him, wondering about the purpose of his visit, when he suddenly asked if I could help him.

A dear friend of his, a 'darling, adorable, simple girl', was arriving from Munich and the reason for his trip to Rome was to fetch her from the station the following morning. The problem was that he had been unable to find lodgings. Could I use my connections with the hotel? (The Hôtel de Russie was an old-fashioned residential hotel, elegant and quiet, with lovely suites looking out over the gardens of the Pincio.) I heard myself saying that I would certainly try, but the manager proved to be out. We decided that I would go to my rehearsal the next morning and Stokowski would fetch the simple, adorable one; after which we would meet in my suite and tackle the problem again.

When I returned to the hotel the following morning it slipped my mind, possibly because I was exhausted after a three-hour rehearsal, that I had told the porter he could let Mr Allen into my suite if he arrived before me. So I was startled, on coming into the sitting-room, to find Stokowski sunk into the sofa with a lady next to him. She wore an outsize raincoat, a broad-brimmed slouch hat over a pair of enormous dark glasses, and flat shoes. I was introduced as 'my dear friend and Maestro', she as 'darling, sweet Miss Gustavson'. The only exposed part of her body was the tip of her nose and a pair of pale lips. Her voice was deep and melodious.

She gave me the shortest possible look and went over to the window to admire the view. Very anxious to solve the problem of their lodgings, I asked the manager to come up. He was a thin little man, with a pale unhealthy face and dark moustaches that pointed upwards. He dressed in a close-fitting morning coat with a silvery tie. After many years of dealing with foreigners, he could make concessions to several languages, though with a most individual delivery. Stokowski, at his most theatrical, moved the servile creature to such a point that it was agreed that an empty room connected with my suite should be furnished to accommodate my friends. The only snag was that they had to share my bathroom. Stokowski was delighted. He thanked me effusively for my generosity and promised that they would be most unobtrusive and would do everything possible not to distract me. They both knew, he said, being professionals themselves, the demands on an artist when he is performing. Miss Gustavson continued to look out of the window.

I said they must have lunch with me. The manager, puzzled but endlessly accommodating, bowed his way out, and in no time at all a table was being laid in my sitting-room and the head waiter with menus and a wine list was standing by to take our order. Stokowski was enchanted. He took several very deep breaths and launched into a eulogy of Graeco-Roman civilisation.

Miss Gustavson then took off her raincoat and hat. She was wearing a tweed skirt and a loose rollneck jersey that emphasised her pale face and her profile. As the Garbo profile was arguably the most celebrated image in the entire history of the cinema, the

'Miss Gustavson' persona seemed suddenly a little transparent. It is one thing to be told that the Eiffel Tower is in fact St Pancras Station, but quite another to believe it.

We sat down at the table, the head waiter in attendance. The bill of fare was full of variety and as the others seemed somewhat hesitant, to speed our selection I made a few suggestions. They drew no response. After a while Miss Gustavson decided she would like some salmon, which was at least progress even if salmon was almost the only thing not listed on the menu. The head waiter asked permission to rush to the restaurant to inquire if some salmon could be found, came back breathlessly to report that it could, and some fifteen minutes later reappeared with a silver tray on which was balanced a beautiful fish with parsley sticking out of its mouth. By that stage I would have settled for anything that merely constituted a decision, so when there were cries of admiration I began to believe in myself again as a host. Only for a moment. Miss Gustavson changed her mind. She told me that people ate too much, and that she would rather have some raw carrots, celery and 'those delicious small tomatoes' that tasted so good in the Mediterranean countries. My heart sank. This was 1938, before the Americans had, during the war, started the fashion for eating raw vegetables. At that time in Italy only donkeys were fed on carrots.

Stokowski was easier. He decided on a mutton chop with a green salad and a raspberry syrup with soda. To be courteous, but without enthusiasm, I asked Miss Gustavson if she would like some wine. She told me that French white wine was delicious and good for the health. I proposed a Pouilly Fuissé or Pouilly Fumé, or a dry Chablis 1934.

She asked me if it was really dry. The head waiter confirmed that it was indeed a dry wine. As she seemed a little doubtful he went down to the restaurant again to consult the *sommelier*. He returned with a broad smile to announce that the vintage was a particularly excellent dry wine. Miss Gustavson then, surprisingly, said she didn't like dry wines and she would rather have, in a jug, a mixture of peaches, pineapple, oranges and any other type of exotic fruit.

At the end of the luncheon I was a spent force. It was late in the afternoon, I had had no rest and my second rehearsal was about to start.

When I got back to the hotel, my principal concern was to avoid meeting them, so I went straight to the restaurant to have a frugal supper in peace before going to bed. When I went upstairs, I opened the sitting-room door cautiously, anxious not to make any noise. There they were, waiting to say goodnight. As we had to share the bathroom there was a protracted charade of artificial politeness: 'Ladies first' – 'Never, you have been working' – 'Oh no, you are my guests' – Never, you are the Maestro.' All this took place while we were holding our toothbrushes. We eventually said goodnight and I went to bed in a daze.

The next day was a holiday. Not having a rehearsal I accepted Stokowski's invitation to luncheon at a *trattoria* near Frascati recommended by a trombone-player of the Philadelphia Orchestra. Stokowski said he was told that the place was enchanting (enraptured gesture of both arms) and that the speciality was 'lingueeeeenie' (outstretched right palm conveying soothing properties of the pasta).

When we went downstairs to leave the hotel, it was apparent that Miss Gustavson's cat was out of its Scandinavian bag. Already in the morning I had sensed a certain tension – maids coming in repeatedly to change towels unnecessarily, waiters returning to collect trays previously fetched, bellboys knocking at the door unsummoned. When the lift gates opened at the ground floor, an army of photographers camped in the hall loosed off a barrage of flashes. Miss Gustavson, wrapped in her usual trench-coat, masked by dark glasses and slouch hat, was hardly visible. Stokowski, wearing his light blue suit, pink socks, pink tie and yellow gloves, was all too visible – but indifferent.

It was a beautiful warm day. We sat on the *trattoria* terrace, gazing down on Rome. Stokowski, feeling very pagan, thought of

CARO Signore e Maestro

    I am coming to Rome on Thursday (24th) afternoon — May I see you? I shall go straight to your Hotel di la Russie —. Unfortunately I must leave about 11 o'clock that night — I shall be so happy to see you again — — (Let's go to Franceschini !!)

        Always sincerely

Echoes of the Gustavson saga: a letter to MF from Leopold Stokowski.

Apollo; Miss Gustavson rested her chin on her fist and looked to be thinking of nothing.

The owner welcomed us eagerly when we mentioned the name of the trombone-player from the Philadelphia Orchestra, but his excitement diminished considerably when the orders were placed: raw carrots with a tomato juice, and an overcooked portion of *linguini* without seasoning, accompanied by a large cup of Italian coffee diluted with hot water. He must have thought it a deliberate insult to the traditions of Nero, Tiberius and the trombone-player.

We returned to the hotel after stopping at Franceschini's, Stokowski's shirtmaker, and at a fashionable milliner's where Miss Gustavson tried – unsuccessfully – to find a gondolier's hat with red streamers. They were both enchanted by the outing, and Stokowski spoke about his great desire to see the place that had been the inspiration for the Gardens of Klingsor in *Parsifal*. I felt this was my cue. I immediately made some telephone calls to help them on their way.

They left the following day. The parting was warm, even affectionate. After saying goodbye to Stokowski, I kissed Miss Gustavson's hand. But I never told her that I knew who she was. Nor that I wanted to be alone.

I was happy in America, and I had the feeling that Nazism was soon to plunge Europe into war; I only needed a resident visa to be able to establish my home in the United States. I expressed this wish to Arthur Judson, my manager, who accepted a series of concerts I had been offered by the Havana Philharmonic, thus making it possible for me to return from Cuba on a permanent Italian visa. So it was that on a bitterly cold January morning I sailed from New York and four days later landed in Cuba.

I was taken by two gentlemen dressed in white drill suits to the Sevilla Hotel in the centre of the city. Sipping a cooling daiquiri (I was unwisely wearing a heavy tweed coat on a very hot day), I inquired about the orchestra, and about the colleagues who had preceded me. I was told that Stokowski had been there a few weeks before and had had a great success. Reassured by this news, I met the orchestra at ten the following morning in optimistic mood. Although some members were exceptional, it was far from good. In the woodwind and brass they all wore uniforms, as they belonged to different bands – Army, Navy, Police and Fire Department. The string section was large, with amateurs in it, but they were all enthusiastic and willing to make music. I was pleased at their alertness, by the commendable effort they had made to study their parts before the first rehearsal, and by having at my disposal the gigantic orchestra necessary for *Till Eulenspiegel*. Alas, at the next rehearsal I faced only a scattered group of players – a few violins, one 'cello, a huge and unnecessary number of grumbling string basses, a couple of heavy brasses, one horn, and the E-flat clarinet, so delighted to play the prankish part of the leading role that nobody could keep him quiet. All this was a disaster. I stressed the necessity, in future, of having the complete orchestra to hand, but was told that the men had other jobs and that they had come to the first rehearsal solely to see the face of the new conductor, and would come to the last for love of music. Poorly paid by the Philharmonic Organisation, they made their living by playing in hotels, radio stations, bands, and by teaching; in their spare time they joined the Symphony Orchestra for the fortnightly concert. I was disappointed, but I persevered. The concerts were a success and I was appointed musical director and conductor.

Looking back at the programmes of those faraway days, I now find them much too ambitious for the capabilities of the orchestra I had at my disposal. My eagerness to experiment with unfamiliar repertoire prompted me to try out technically difficult works at a stage when the orchestra still needed a more basic training. However, the first season ended successfully, and I was granted a larger budget to improve further weaknesses. Unable to find a leader for the first violin section amongst the locals, in New York I engaged a brilliant musician, Orlando Barera, as concert master and assistant conductor. Son of a well-known violin teacher at the Bologna Conservatory, he had a plain, straightforward approach in disciplining inexperienced players. I knew that his personal charm would win the confidence of the men, and his help, combined with two more acquisitions from the United States – a principal 'cellist and a first oboe – would contribute significantly to the betterment of the orchestra.

During the four years I spent in Havana the musical life evolved immensely. Under the sponsorship of the Philharmonic, Paul Csonka, an Austrian refugee, organised a chorus that enabled us to perform Beethoven's Ninth Symphony, Verdi's *Requiem*, Kodaly's *Psalmus Hungaricus*. and other choral works never presented to that public before. Famous soloists appeared with us – Heifetz, Emmanuel Feuermann, Artur Rubinstein, and many others. The house was sold out by subscription, and some concerts were repeated at the more spacious Opera House at popular prices. Although the war was on – Cuba had joined the Allies in the conflict – music was flourishing. I was happy at last to have the opportunity of conducting a.large repertoire which my previous globe-trotting guest-engagements had denied me, and to be able, in spite of my alien nationality, to carry on my work undisturbed.

For me, the first year of the war had been one of desperate indecision. For long periods I had lived abroad, away from Italy and from the Fascist political movement which I had admired when I was fourteen years old as the saviour of Italy from anarchy and Communism, and which I now detested. I disliked the alliance with Nazism and I had no faith in the hysterical multitudes swearing allegiance to Mussolini. Nevertheless, it was my country of birth, now at war. It was a conflict of ideas: my feelings were all for a democratic world, but at the same time I was torn by a sense of loyalty to the land of my forefathers.

I eventually took a definite stand. I conducted a benefit concert for the Cuban-American Allied Relief Fund. Count Sforza, a leading anti-Fascist who became Prime Minister after the war, delivered an important political speech in the interval. I was relieved to have taken a decision whose making had harassed me for so long. I was now officially on the side of the Allies. My prominent public position as conductor of the Philharmonic drew retaliation from Nazi-Fascist factions for having endorsed the Allied cause, and I was continuously threatened by them.

I would forgive Cuba all my professional vicissitudes simply for the fact that it was because of my sojourn there that I met my wife, Nena. A few weeks after the opening of my first season, the President of the Philharmonic board, Señor Batista (no relation of the dictator), gave a dinner party in his house in my honour. My attention was caught at once by a young lady who had just returned from Europe. Her name was Maria Luisa (Nena) Azpiazu, of Basque descent on her father's side and Catalonian on her mother's. After a short marriage she had come back to live at her parents' home in Cuba with her small daughter – at that time in Cuba it was not proper for a young woman to live alone. I was captivated at our first meeting and we soon became inseparable. We married in 1945 and we are inseparable still.

Nena attracted to her house not only the social set, but also painters, writers and musicians. One of her childhood friends I came to regard as part of my family. This was the remarkable Fifi Tarafa, who owned 'Central Cuba', a sugar mill two hours' drive from Havana, and who devoted most of her life and fortune to her country.

One of the regular visitors to the Floridita (a bar in Havana) was Ernest Hemingway. He would sit, far from sober, at a marble table listening attentively to Basque stories told by *pelotarios*. He liked the Basque race; he thought they had strong and interesting characteristics, and he once told my wife that he would eventually like to write a book on the *Euzko*. On many occasions he asked me to his house – he lived in a *finca* in a village near Havana. The walls of the rooms were covered by posters advertising *corridas, toreros,* the floors were fitted with a thick rope matting, and everybody walked barefooted. One had the feeling that his main passion was drinking martinis or pineapple juice with gin, the second was fishing, and the third was the Spanish language. He once told me that the secret of his success as a writer was thinking in Spanish and translating into English, and there is about the Hemingway style the clear-cut poetical vitality that one also finds in the Spanish race. He was always interested in people, in nature, in places. He was an amazing listener, with a powerful perception of what was happening around him, which he stored and used in his writings. His appearance and language was that of a 'tough guy', but I suspected that he was a softy with a sense of insecurity. I recall him sitting on his bed, legs crossed and barefoot, telling a group of friends of the killing of his first bear, when he was a boy. He burst into tears and sobbed for a long time.

At the end of my fourth season the Havana Philharmonic Orchestra had greatly improved, but my relations with the board of directors had much deteriorated. I was restless and tired of the perennially beautiful weather; I felt the lack of competition, the need to hear other orchestras, other conductors. I wanted to move, to return to the United States, not to remain stagnant in one place for too long. Through some good friends in the American Embassy, I was granted a special visa to return to New York. I was delighted, although I knew the Army Draft Board was waiting for me at the other end.

When I arrived in New York I neatly packed away my suits in mothballs and presented myself to the recruiting service, perfectly certain that from then on the Army would take care of my food, clothing and lodgings. A few days later, on a brisk early morning, I stood in front of a mid-Manhattan building in the company of a crowd of men of the most varied types. Punctually at 6 a.m. a door was opened by two uniformed G.I.s, waving a sample of the card which summoned us. 'Keep this in your right hand, and no pushing'.

Our first stop was a large hall. The authoritative voice of a sergeant gave us the order to strip completely and to make a neat bundle of our clothes, which would be found eventually at the exit. A flow of coarse jokes came out of the human herd, quickly controlled by a 'You guys shut up!' from the sergeant in command. To find myself naked, with a chain holding a large piece of white cardboard dangling on my back, gave me a profound feeling of humiliation. I felt ridiculous and, not knowing what to do, remained motionless until a uniformed man pushed me roughly towards a very long corridor. Following a single line, we were led one at a time into small unpainted plywood cabins. In each of them we were confronted by two examining doctors. The first cubicle was for a superficial check-up for major physical defects – missing limbs and the like – which did not last long, and I was rapidly dismissed after they had written on the white cardboard, I suppose, that nothing was missing. The second session took longer as it was a chemical analysis, with blood tests and so on. I had to stand for quite a while before the results were written on the chart, and wait until a six-foot-tall muscular hulk, who had fainted at the sight of his own blood, was revived. We were then herded to the third cabin for a complete X-ray.

Everything moved smoothly, and in relative silence. A few short questions were asked, in a detached way, without ever meeting the eyes of the draftee. It must have already been afternoon when I reached the office of the general practitioner, as the sun was beating on the opposite side of the building. I was extremely tired after having gone through so many tests, dentistry, nose and throat, oculist, tossed around like a steer in the market. My mind was blurred: I felt as if I had completely lost my personality and that my only identity was the as yet unknown to me appraisal written on my back. The general practitioner sat at his desk studying the report on my numerous tests. He then leant back, stretched his arms upwards, stared at the ceiling and asked me some questions. His voice was disagreeable, with a nasal manner of speaking – I guessed from the Middle West. If I found *his* voice unattractive, my foreign 'Continental-English' accent also rubbed him up the wrong way. His face became purple. Glaring at me, he said sarcastically 'We will beat it out of you, that phoney talk of yours!' He then grabbed a stethoscope and a little hammer, and made further tests. While he was writing his verdict on my back, I stood looking at my toes dejectedly.

I left his cabin more upset than ever. Standing for hours, morally weary after the protracted ordeal I had had to endure, I felt that fate was bent on destroying me. In this painful state of mind, I crossed the threshold of a nicely furnished room, with a comfortable chair in front of a desk. A middle-aged gentleman in civilian clothes – in marked contrast to the white tunics – walked towards me and greeted me with warmth. He had a deep mellow voice and he addressed me as 'Maestro'. He begged me to sit down, after offering me a towelling bathrobe. He told me that he had heard me conducting the Philharmonic and that he had much enjoyed my performance of *Daphnis and Chloe*, and my sensitive rendition of Brahms's First Symphony. In a few minutes I had melted completely, conquered by his cordiality and charm. We talked about art, about Europe. He seemed very interested in my conversation, looking at me straight in the eye, with a faint but engaging smile. Our chat had already lasted about fifteen minutes when he abruptly asked me 'Do you get nervous before a performance?' I said, 'Yes, I always feel as if I had a knot in my solar plexus.' I hadn't finished my sentence before the warm, friendly, sensitive expression on his face quite evaporated. He asked me to hang the bathrobe on a hook and dismissed me with a nod, after writing the final judgement. In the next room two officers gave me a card with my classification. I was rejected. My bundle of clothes was returned to me, and in no time I was in the street, walking towards my hotel.

It was four in the afternoon: I was famished, exhausted, mystified by the result of my physical examination. I was then a little over thirty, in perfect health, and I hadn't fainted at the sight of my own blood like the man in front of me (who was, incidentally, drafted). After reviewing the whole day's ordeal, I came to the conclusion that I had horrified the psychoanalyst when I mentioned my solar plexus.

We Europeans are in the habit of discussing medicine with our family doctor; the French know all about the stomach's malfunction, the Italians about liver ailments. But this empiric medical knowledge was highly suspicious to the psychoanalyst. 'This man is a neurotic, a liability to the US Army.' I felt insulted; but I am afraid that he was right.

After I left Cuba, Erich Kleiber succeeded me as conductor of the Havana Philharmonic. A few months later I was offered the New Orleans Symphony. If this was not the orchestra for which I had yearned – every young conductor wants the Boston, New York or Philadelphia – I was lucky to get a job while the war was on, and while I was still an enemy alien.

I remained in charge of the Symphony Orchestra for eight years, spending six months from October to April in New Orleans, except for guest engagements in other cities. This was probably not the most exciting period of my life; but thanks to my wife's warmth and hospitality many people visited us, usually for supper after the weekly concerts. Tennessee Williams was a frequent visitor. We asked him first to our house because Rubinstein's wife, Nella, wanted to meet him. He was always accompanied by his uncle, an Episcopalian bishop, but I cannot say that at a party he was an asset. He smoked countless cigarettes through a long black holder, and seldom contributed to the conversation.

Artur Rubinstein's annual visit as soloist with the orchestra was an event. Apart from his playing, his personality, amusing tales and witty remarks broke the monotony of a provincial city's lethargic routine and put us in touch once again with

Nena in Pennsylvania, 1941.

MF and Artur Rubinstein after a concert: New Orleans, 1946.

the outside world. All our soloists contributed to this form of diversion with their various idiosyncrasies. Some arrived at the last moment before the final rehearsal and kept the management on tenterhooks. Those who were neurotics told you they felt they could not play, but if you told them to keep calm because you could replace their concert with a symphony just performed on tour the week before, they immediately decided to play. Others were on a diet, but actually hoped to be asked to a meal, for some real home cooking. There were soloists who were nuisances, taking all the rehearsal time they could get, and giving a poor performance in return. Some had a quick sense of humour. A well-known Jewish pianist, Oscar Levant, after hitting a number of wrong notes, whispered to me, 'This Steinway piano is anti-Semitic.'

The monotonous years in New Orleans were interrupted in the summer months by our vacation in northern Connecticut. Arrowhill, our country place, was on top of a hill. One could look down the valley to fields of clover and corn untidily divided by stone walls. It was an old farmhouse built in the 1760s by early settlers who had abandoned it for the more promising West.

We had two hundred and fifty acres of land, and in the wooded part we could still find the remains of cottages with kitchen utensils abandoned on a brick stove, not yet completely destroyed by time. A large barn was attached to the house, stripped of the boards that once upheld the hayloft; this became a big music room with excellent acoustics. The surrounding land had the charm and freedom of a country where the hand of man had not made careful order.

Old Commander Hinckley, our nearest neighbour, lived a mile away. He had erected a huge mast near the house – a sentimental reminder of his days on board ship, now used for hoisting a flag with a martini glass embroidered on it to signal his friends that it was drinking time. He was tall and corpulent, with a corrugated face, the consequence of exposure to foul weather at sea. He always wore a blazer and a captain's cap, from the back of which some thin blondish hair escaped. We never knew if his vacillating walk was due to many years at sea or to many tots of gin.

To the left of our house, down a lonely country lane, lived Bob Grant, a Bostonian who had spent most of his life in London as president of an American bank. His wife Priscilla, also a Bostonian, spent her days cutting branches, pruning trees, trimming flowers and tossing manure. They had exchanged a worldly life in London for one of comfortable simplicity on retirement. Their English friends came to visit them every year. We enjoyed seeing

Nena and MF at Arrowhill.

the Grants and became quite close, and as our land was adjacent together we restocked it with birds – I for the pleasure of watching them, he to atone for all the grouse he had shot in Scotland.

From Arrowhill it was forty miles along winding roads to Tanglewood in Massachussets where the Boston Symphony Orchestra performed twice a week to an audience of thousands. The Tanglewood estate had been donated by a rich Bostonian to provide the site for a festival. A huge dale gave the appearance of an amphitheatre, with a shell at the bottom to accommodate the players. The acoustics were adequate. The property was dotted with cottages owned or rented by rich music lovers who entertained guest artists and gave a social atmosphere to the festival. As many musicians lived in that part of New England, it was a pleasant and stimulating meeting place.

Serge Koussewitzky was the high priest, and with his Boston Symphony Orchestra provided some spectacular performances of his favourite, mostly Russian, repertoire. His interpretations of Tchaikovsky symphonies were remarkable, his conceit and his pomposity boundless. On the day of the concert his limousine was escorted by two motorcycles in front and by a flashing police car at the back, to cover the few yards that divided his cottage from the backstage dressing-room. He would acknowledge with a paternal gesture the applause of his admirers lining both sides of the lane. He invariably wore a black cape over his impeccably-cut morning coat.

We were often invited to tea at his house after the concert. A life-size painting of the Maestro playing double bass occupied one entire wall of his drawing-room, and underneath it, on an armchair, he sat supreme, accepting the most outrageous flattery from his guests. As he knew that I often saw Toscanini, he invariably asked me: 'Comment va-t-il, le pauvre vieux – il paraît qu'il oublie tout.' Toscanini on Koussewitzky was more direct. He used to tell me 'That fool should stop conducting.' Madame Koussewitzky, a niece of his first wife, a pale lady straight out of a Chekhov play, moved around amongst the guests serving tea and keeping a sharp eye on the scene in order to replace the person talking to her husband whenever the Maestro began to show signs of boredom.

On Koussewitzky's retirement, the Russian influence was succeeded by a more frivolous French virtuosity with the advent of Charles Munch. Not being able to hear his concerts in winter because of my own commitments, I enjoyed attending his performances at Tanglewood. I ws fascinated by his personality, charm and erratic artistry; his brilliant improvisations had a touch of genius. I have never heard a greater variety of tempi, sounds and ideas in the same piece on three successive days. His fantasy created moments of frenzied exaltation in Berlioz's *Fantastic* Symphony and voluptuous passions in the *Romeo and Juliet* love scene. Carried away by his imagination, he went to the limits of the technical possibilities of an orchestra, driving the players to achieve wild effects. Many years later, when I invited him to conduct my orchestra in Rome, I had the opportunity of analysing his way of rehearsing. He did not go into details: he generally read through a piece, emphasising salient points, teasing the orchestra with his capricious beat. I felt he deliberately confused the players to keep them on tenterhooks

The concerts remained popular. The young camped by the thousand along the ridge at the head of the slope, picnicking, listening to music, making love. The elderly audience sat on stalls near the shell. Many great artists who had retired attended the festival. I remember once sitting behind Fritz Kreisler at a concert in which Zino Francescatti was the soloist. Kreisler had forgotten his hearing aid and was frantically asking his wife Harriet if she had a spare one in her bag. A gentleman sitting next to her, overhearing the conversation, offered his own to Kreisler who accepted it, unconcerned at depriving its donor of hearing the performance. At the end of the concert Kreisler returned the apparatus to his wife who passed it on to the generous music lover, saying 'I am so sorry that you could not hear Francescatti.' The reply was: 'Yes, but I had such joy watching the Maestro's face while he was listening.'

In 1952 I left the New Orleans Symphony for the Baltimore Symphony. The Lyric Theatre there leans towards the nostalgic – I have been told that the hall is a copy of the Gewandhaus in Leipzig. The building is unattractive on the outside, but the interior forms one of the best concert halls in which I have ever performed. The acoustics are splendid, and the hall has the civilised and intimate aspect of an old-fashioned *Konzertsaal*. I enjoyed working in the Lyric and looked forward each season to performing there. With two important universities, Princeton in New Jersey and Howard in Washington, not too far away, I had the chance of engaging their excellent choirs, and the proximity of New York meant I could secure actors such as Basil Rathbone and Sir Cedric Hardwicke – to take part in, respectively, Schumann's *Manfred* and Honegger's *King David*. In the United States, unlike Europe (with a few exceptions), the permanent

126

Rosa Ponselle, squirrel and MF: Baltimore, 1963.

conductor had total control over the choice of programmes and the difficult task of seeking variety for them. I often had to resort to performing operas in concert form, engaging local young singers for minor parts as support for the celebrated ones in leading roles.

I frequently found talented young people to collaborate with the symphony orchestra among the pupils of Rosa Ponselle. Her real Neapolitan name was Rosa Ponzillo and she lived in a sumptuous villa built high on a hill overlooking the fashionable Green Spring Valley on the outskirts of Baltimore. After her retirement from the stage she settled there in a home appropriate to a famous diva, travelling only to Washington to sing for President Eisenhower on his inauguration day. Her past glories brought a steady flow of admirers on pilgrimage from far and wide, or students seeking counsel, many of them remaining under her guidance to perfect their studies. This holy place was called Villa Pace. She may have longed for peace after a hectic career, but the visitor to the villa met with exactly its opposite. The barking of five Dalmatians set the alarm for thirteen toy poodles to leap out of their baskets towards the door, yapping and protesting. They were all named after operatic characters,

127

and in the happy confusion created by the bell Escamillo might jump on top of Violetta, Norma do her necessities on the entrance rug, Don Giovanni lift his hind leg, Carmen bite Aïda's ears, while the more timid ones, Micaela, Santuzza, Gilda, Alfredo, Manrico and others, clamoured prudently from the top of the stairs, their heads sticking out between the banisters. Added to the medley were the vocalisms of various pupils exercising their lungs in different rooms before facing the diva for a lesson, and the shrieks of four squirrels vaulting madly in their cage, eager to join in the commotion.

In the reception room Rosa would be coaching a young tenor, conducting the accompanist at the piano with her left arm while the right suggested to the singer where he should rest his voice. She would point to her stomach for the chest tones or the roof of her mouth for high notes. Rosa had unique vocal gifts; she was as much at ease in *Carmen* as in Violetta's role. The range of her voice was extraordinary, with an even and effortless beauty in every register. She belonged to the golden era of the Metropolitan Opera, sharing the stage with Caruso, Titta Ruffo, Scotti and other deities of *bel canto*.

I arrived in America a decade too late for the epoch of the star. The Metropolitan Opera had gone into decline, Stokowski had resigned from the Philadelphia Orchestra, Toscanini had just left the glamorous Philharmonic to conduct the NBC Symphony in a broadcasting studio, the Hollywood gods of the silent film when obliged to speak were tumbling from their Olympian summits. Furthermore a democratic era in art was beginning, and the autocracy of the star was already vanishing. But Rosa even in private life was always a great star. I recall once when both we and Elizabeth Schwarzkopf were invited for supper at Rosa's, after our concert in Baltimore. Elizabeth was thrilled to meet the famous diva of the Twenties. Rosa sang, her voice was still beautiful, she told anecdotes of her career, she was in superb form, and at four in the morning we were all still there.

In our present world of fewer contrasts and less individualism,

Rosa Ponselle as Norma, New York.

it is intriguing to talk to a person who remembers an age when every form of expression was more dramatic. Rosa's grandiose gestures and attitudes were appropriate to her epoch – a world of no restraints, of abundance and unreality, of the splendour and prodigality of a Cecil B. de Mille production. Rosa characterised her roles with overwhelming intensity, magnifying emotion, stretching the rhetoric of passion to a public demanding such extrovert acting in order to understand and to be convinced. Today's audiences are more sophisticated and feel that exaggerated acting is unacceptable; performances have adopted more subtle techniques. One of the results is a niggardly expression of eloquence that sometimes makes one long for the past. I wonder if today's restraint in performing is not due to a sort of self-protection, a necessary economy to accommodate the artist's exacting schedule. An artist should be able to be selective, and avoid alluring offers that mean rejection of quality in favour of quantity.

Although during my many years in America I had tried deliberately to diminish my links with the Old World, my taste drove me subconsciously towards that which reflected a European sensibility. I have met many American composers and performed their works. I admire Aaron Copland, Walter Piston, Paul Creston and many others for their craftsmanship, but Samuel Barber's music moves me more deeply. I have always found in Barber a European form of expression. He had lived in Europe for a few years, mostly at the American Academy in Rome, and he had studied for a while with Ottorino Respighi. In his *Prayers of Kierkegaard,* or in his *Adagio for Strings*, one feels something more substantial and liberated than the customary skill and efficiency of American composition.

In 1955 I decided to perform the European première of *The Prayers of Kierkegaard* at the opening of the Festwoche in Vienna. The work had not been a success the year before at its

MF *receiving a doctorate from Tulane University, Louisiana, 1950.*

world première with the Boston Symphony Orchestra conducted by Charles Munch, and Barber himself discouraged me from performing it. I liked the piece and was convinced that all it needed was some changes in the score. I told Barber, and he agreed to cut some parts which I thought superfluous, to give new shape to the structure of the composition. *The Prayers of Kierkegaard* was an immediate success in Vienna. The composer, who was present at the performance, was delighted. Some weeks later he came to hear the London première when I conducted it with the London Philharmonic Orchestra at the Festival Hall. Later he wrote to me: 'As a matter of fact, it is practically your composition.'

If I found in Barber a sort of 'consanguinity' I felt in Peter Mennin a fusion of the gifts of the Old and New Worlds. I first met him when he came to hear a rehearsal of his Third Symphony that I was performing in Baltimore, and I was impressed by his direct and sensitive personality. I liked his music. In the lyricism of the second movement I felt the affinity with his father's land, Lucca, that small part of Tuscany that gave birth to such composers as Boccherini, Geminiani, Catalani, and Giacomo Puccini.

I think that in America the vast distances and the intense pace of life prevented me from becoming more intimate with the composers. In twenty-two years I saw Stravinsky only once. He came to our house for dinner while stopping in New Orleans on his way to California. The short notice created havoc. Our negro cook, mistaking Stravinsky for Tchaikovsky, one of whose 'tunes' she had heard, left like a thunderbolt to go to the hairdresser, leaving my wife (an inexperienced cook at that time) alone in the kitchen. She returned as the meal was ending, in a pleated white gown like a Greek maiden, with an ornate hair-do reminiscent of a Euphronios figure on a fifth century B.C. vase, merely to greet the famous guest and to bring a record of Stokowski to be autographed.

I met Gottfried von Einem at one of my concerts in Vienna in 1955 when he came backstage after the Austrian première of Rolf Liebermann's *Concerto for Jazz Band and Symphony Orchestra*. This piece had aroused a certain curiosity amongst the Viennese intellectuals owing to the fact that a jazz band was combining forces with a symphony orchestra, culminating in the last movement in a rousing mambo. I was changing from my tailcoat into a more informal suit when a knock at the door of the artists' room of the Konzerthaus announced a tall young man with wavy tawny hair and a powerful jaw under an aquiline nose. With a warm smile he introduced himself and his wife, a pretty but austere young lady, who I eventually learnt was Bismarck's great-granddaughter. The delicacy of this diaphanous creature was a striking contrast to her husband's exuberance. We engaged in pleasant conversation, with an immediate rapport over our views on modern music. He was unusually candid, but generous and without malice. So enjoyable was our first encounter that it was the beginning of a lasting friendship, and he made me eager to know more of him through his music.

I have since conducted many of his works. The most impressive of his symphonic pieces is, in my opinion, *Stundenlied*, an oratorio with a Bertold Brecht text. I saw him now and then, and we would take up our friendship easily from where we left off. After his wife's death he moved to Berlin for a while and I often met him at Boris Blacher's home.

Blacher I knew by reputation for many years. I admired his sophisticated writing in the *Variations on a Theme of Paganini*, *Studies in Pianissimo* and his *Piano Concerto on a Theme of Clementi*. For this latter piece I recall having engaged Gerty Herzog to play the solo part at one of my concerts in Rome, only to discover by chance that she was Blacher's wife. Whenever I went to conduct in Berlin I was invited to their house, and I was deeply impressed by Blacher's personality, He was frail and sensitive, with small piercing eyes and white thin hair falling on both sides of his lean face. At home he donned an outsize porridge-coloured cablestitch pullover, with nonchalance but chic. His house was not the conventional home of a composer – no piano, no scores, no paper with staves, or books on music – but more that of an ascetic. The furniture was simple and functional, He would sit for hours in an armchair just to think. There he worked. Once when I was visiting him, I ingenuously asked to hear part of the opera he was composing. He took out of a drawer a magnetic tape which consisted of the *glissando* of a trombone. 'This', he said, 'has all the material I need. I now require a good technician to do the splicing.' As an interpreter of 'conventional' music, I was puzzled. He had plunged deep into electronic music and into a world I had not encountered. Not being able to share his feelings, I feared for a moment that our friendship would suffer.

I believe that friendship is made up of mutual interest in two human beings. Consequently all my friendships have been with people of varied habits and tastes and occupations, but there

133

Wilhelm Furtwängler and his wife Elisabeth with (right) Harry de Pauer.

has always been a link of a shared experience which bound us. Naturally, when music is the common language it draws two people together even if their opinions differ. I believe that through the art of von Einem and Blacher I discovered our subconscious affinity, rooted probably in memories of a historical musical period in Germany which had left a deep impression on us. Another old friend is Harry de Pauer. His acquaintances – ranging from Archduchesses to game wardens – are different from mine, but he has such love for Austrian nature, such understanding of a mood when walking the Kärtnerring on a Sunday morning before a Philharmonic concert, that all this links us together.

With the soloists with whom I have worked I feel that friendship springs primarily from the fusion of interpretative thought. I shall always remember, when Artur Rubinstein and I performed Chopin's Concerto in F Minor, the magical beauty of the second movement. We have played various composers together – Beethoven, Brahms, Tchaikovsky, Rachmaninov, de Falla – and on many occasions we may have achieved better overall results; but in that performance there was the harmony of a complete understanding.

I recall other instances with Serkin, Brailowsky, Szigeti and Casadesus when our interpretation accorded with total sympathy, when the pulse of two natures was one. Unforgettable the height of expression Menuhin reaches in the G minor passage in the first movement of Beethoven's concerto. As for Horowitz, making music with him was always a sublime experience. Yet it is strange how difficult this communion of the spirit has been with other artists of great reputation.

My admiration for Heifetz was limitless. We played together many times; he had a celestial purity of tone, a masterly technique and all the gifts of a true virtuoso, but nevertheless I was always perplexed by his interpretations. I always felt as if he had shed the weight of his European background so as to enter lightly into life in the New World. One wonders to what extent an artist's cultural roots affect his performance.

I remember a conversation I had with Casadesus about the public in the United States. We both agreed that it was essential to face a European audience regularly in order to reconsider the validity of our interpretations. The American public is highly demanding, but above all of technical perfection and brilliance. Provided that the fruit is offered nicely wrapped, nobody complains if it is unripe. Music is considered more of an entertainment than an art: many people go to concerts for recreation after a hard day's work and expect to be amused. The performer perceives the apathy of the audience which demands to be excited, and starts to overdo the effects, beginning with the most trivial – that of speed. In America almost every musician performs at a faster tempo because of a subconscious fear of boring the public. This insecurity in the artist requires an adjustment of

Robert Casadesus and MF, Venice, 1951.

interpretation when he finds himself in countries such as Austria or Germany, where the audience has an intellectual and emotional approach rather than a need for physical stimulus. In the world of today how beneficial it is for an artist to take refuge among people whose pace is human, where the rational rhythm has not been distorted, and where nature is friendly, bearable at all seasons. Music is an intimate expression, easily crushed by a brutal environment, by colossal concrete skyscrapers, and above all by the people living in them. On each of my journeys I grew slowly more attached to the Old World, and when I returned to the United States I felt a distinct change in my inner self.

It was in 1925 that three young virtuosi escaped from Russia: Vladimir Horowitz, Nathan Milstein and Gregor Piatigorsky. All three, in their early twenties, were accompanied by a manager, Alexander Merowitch, also a Russian. Their career in the West started with a bang. Horowitz in a few months had Europe at his feet; Milstein, after playing Dvorak's violin concerto with the Berlin Philharmonic under Furtwängler, was in demand everywhere; Piatigorsky, principal 'cellist with the Berlin Philharmonic, became internationally known as well. With the success of his three boys Merowitch's ego got out of control, and he firmly believed that they were playing only through his hypnotic power and managerial acumen.

I met him in Berlin through one of his admirers, Lida Piatigorsky (then Piatigorsky's wife, later Madame Pierre Fournier). Knowing that at that time I was at the beginning of my career, she thought I could benefit from his advice. She arranged a meeting for me at his suite at the Adlon Hotel.

He was wearing a silk top hat and a blue and red Chinese gown over a formal suit. He was then in his late forties, tall, broad and sturdy, with a large head deeply set into his torso as if he had no neck. His small slanting eyes were shrewd, and his fleshy flat nose looked like the nose of a boxer bashed by innumerable blows. He had a curious heavy way of walking which made him look like a neatly-dressed Neanderthal Man.

He courteously invited me to sit on a sofa and then began to walk back and forth in the room, talking incessantly about the strategy of how to 'build a career'. I listened resignedly for a while until, tired of turning my head left to right and right to left in order to follow his marathon, I decided to concentrate on an inanimate object in front of me.

I can only recollect that his 'strategy' consisted of organising a 'peripheral attack', and I remember that the names of Napoleon, Wellington and Blücher came up regularly in his oration. I left exhausted. A few months later I heard that he had been committed to a lunatic asylum.

I met him again a few years afterwards in New York, in the interval of a concert at Carnegie Hall. He had regained his sanity but had lost his three artists. They maintained a cordial friendship, but had left him for other managements. I occasionally met him at musician friends' houses and I enjoyed listening to his anecdotes which were always colourful and amusing, although I always suspected that most of them were the product of a fervid imagination.

One of his stories, which was confirmed by Wanda Horowitz concerned a night out in a German city. It seems that Horowitz and a few friends had decided to visit the clubs and cabarets in the town. The last stop was a fashionable establishment where *filles de joie*, scantily dressed, paraded on a stage. Their over-painted lips, flaming wigs, naked bosoms and short skirts of ostrich feathers were typical of pre-Second World War taste in Germany. When the show was over, Horowitz, who had spotted a piano in a corner of the room, dashed towards it, opened the lid and began to play. His success was instantaneous. The ladies rushed to gather round him, and as Horowitz seemed to be occupying their complete attention, the madame decided that the only thing to do was to close the establishment and to listen.

The next day was Horowitz's concert. When he walked on stage he saw, sitting in a box, the madame surrounded by her girls. They were dressed in their finest and loudest clothes, and as he approached the piano they all leant forward to cheer and applaud.

After the war, when I resumed my concerts in Europe, I engaged Merowitch as my personal representative. He had the unusual quality of patience with artists' problems. He could cope with the usual indecisions when drawing up programmes: 'Should I close the concert with a Chopin *Polonaise* or Stravinsky's *Petrushka*?' or 'Which encore is more effective when played first?' The arguments that go on for hours with every performance.

Merowitch oozed comforting serenity before a concert. He would sit quietly in the green room not saying a word, with his hands on his knees and an impassive look in his eyes. Just before walking on stage he would rise and say in his deep voice: '*Poydgem.*' 'Let's go.'

He travelled with us for four years. In 1957 the London Philharmonic sent Wilfrid van Wyck to see me in Baltimore to negotiate my becoming their permanent conductor. My reluctance to talk business (at that moment I was preparing Beethoven's Ninth Symphony for the last concert of the season, and also my beloved stepdaughter Maria Luisa was getting married) prompted me to send Merowitch to London with my conditions, which were almost identical with their offer. A few days later a cable from the London Philharmonic regretted my 'unacceptable terms' but looked forward to a series of concerts with them in London and on tour. It was signed by Eric Bravington. Some weeks later my wife, Merowitch and I left on the *Queen Elizabeth* for England.

It was on the second day out, while we were walking on deck, that I noticed that he was highly excited. He was pacing up and down recounting the most fantastic tales. I listened nervously, trying to conceal my apprehension. Two days later Lionel Carine, the purser, asked me for a drink in his quarters and, after a short desultory conversation, produced the ship's log where all the events on board were carefully recorded. He began to read with a monotonous voice: 'Mr Merowitch called the cabin steward the night before and ordered him to kneel at his feet saying that he, Mr Merowitch, was the Tsar. He then summoned the head waiter at the grill to his presence and ordered a special menu for the following day, which was Russian Easter. It consisted of a pastry reproduction of the Kremlin filled with masses of caviar, and of hard-boiled eggs in their multi-coloured painted shells.'

Carine stopped reading and looked at me, saying: 'Very odd fellow, your secretary. I am afraid that I must have a psychiatrist on board when we reach Southampton before allowing him to disembark.' The psychiatrist found him perfectly normal – indeed he said he had enjoyed a most interesting conversation with him.

In London the next day, Mr Schwenter, the manager of the Ritz Hotel, called to inform me that Mr Merowitch had torn off the tailcoat of a waiter, had asked the Ukrainian hairdresser to kneel in front of him, and had smashed a looking-glass. Mr

Schwenter was apologetic, but he felt he had to call for medical help to have him taken away. I asked him to be patient and wait for Mrs Merowitch's arrival from New York the following day. My wife had already telephoned Milstein's wife Thérèse, who said she had suspected something was wrong with Merowitch when he had come to say goodbye to them before leaving New York with us. She and Wanda Toscanini Horowitz immediately arranged Mrs Merowitch's flight to London.

In the meantime Merowitch had cancelled all my engagements on the Continent, and I had to reassure all the managers that there was nothing wrong with me and that I could fulfil all my commitments. His wife succeeded in taking him back to America, though she left with a black eye after he had accused her of being Stalin's mistress. It was then that Eric Bravington told me that Merowitch had told the London Philharmonic that I would not become their conductor unless he, Merowitch, became their manager.

When I next saw Nathan Milstein, his only comment was 'I told you so.'

In general I have never become comfortably familiar with conductors. Not, I think, because of any antipathy on my part; I have always been friendly, ready to appreciate their qualities, and have tried to help when in a position to do so. For my taste, however, I have found most of them too conceited, mistrustful and even occasionally vicious. I have never been able to tolerate people who *demand* veneration. If Sir Thomas Beecham had not possessed a keen wit he would have been insufferable. His poses and his pretentions emphasised his pomposity in every attitude he took. But his sense of humour saved him. I recall his negotiations with the manager of the Baltimore Symphony Orchestra when I was its music director and had invited him to conduct. They were long and ludicrous. His secretary wrote interminable letters to the manager, to make sure that Sir Thomas would be treated with proper reverence, that the committee would receive him at the station, that a limousine would await him at the hotel, and that rehearsals would take place at a certain hour. As I cannot bear people putting themselves on pedestals, I reluctantly paid him a visit before the first rehearsal in order to introduce him to the orchestra. To my few words of welcome to Baltimore (Wallis Simpson's birthplace), he replied 'My dear Maestro, I am delighted to be in the city that gave birth to the woman who almost wrecked the British Empire.'

For some reason I never appreciated Sir Thomas's conducting. I always found his artistry superficial, a sort of musicality enjoying external effects with no relation to inner emotion. I have heard him in concerts and in two operas, *Tristan and Isolde* and *Carmen*. Yet not once have I been touched by his performances. I have always felt that he was a narrator rather than an interpreter. He had a remarkable gift of leadership, but lacked the capacity for reacting to emotion which enables a performer to project suffering or passion.

Furtwängler's artistry had a peculiar magic. A tall, thin man, with a scraggy neck, a high forehead, two piercing blue eyes peering from beneath bushy eyebrows, and long arms with expressive hands, he had an amazing physical grip on the public. His quivering beat (a sort of insecurity in his technique) and his delayed action in attack transmitted to the audience an extraordinary tension. He could create breathtaking effects in the slow movements particularly. The transition between the scherzo and the finale in Schumann's Fourth will remain in my mind as one of the most magical moments. The feeling of suspense that he achieved during the fifty bars before reaching the majestic chords of the finale of Beethoven's Fifth, holding a ravishing *pianissimo* on the strings, the soft sound of the timpani like a feeble heartbeat, the first violins whispering without *vibrato* – it was sheer enchantment. Nor could one easily forget the celestial atmosphere he created with the orchestra in the closing bars of *Meistersinger*'s second act. He had in his music a strong feeling of compassion, a sense of resignation that made his Brahms Third Symphony memorable. I have never heard a better introduction to the third act of *Tristan*. The deep, sinking sensation in the low strings, the sense of despair, of gloom, while the rising theme in the first violins gives a hint of hope eventually to plunge again into hopelessness. It was utter mastery.

In spite of all this, his rehearsals were boring. He never had the indisputable technical command that so much impresses the orchestra. A few years ago an intimate friend of his told me that Furtwängler had once confessed his regret that he was not feared and respected like Toscanini. German conductors never had the virtuosity of a Toscanini or a De Sabata at rehearsals. De Sabata's control of an orchestra was supreme. His was a technical *tour de force,* correcting the intonation with total accuracy, sometimes playing different instruments himself in order to demonstrate the phrasing, showing off his prodigious memory, and galvanising the players by a personal display of sheer talent. I have a far more vivid recollection of his rehearsals than I do of his performances. I remember an extraordinary one of Wagner's Good Friday music from *Parsifal* and Respighi's *Pines of Rome* with the Santa Cecilia Orchestra, when he obtained the utmost in beautiful sonorities from his players. The performance on the day of the concert was not as good. I also recall an explosive performance of the first act of *Othello* at the Vienna Opera, and a superb *Tosca* at La Scala. De Sabata was flamboyant and theatrical. I admired his great skill, but I felt disturbed by his flashy virtuosity. Looking back to those far-off days, it was Furtwängler who gave me more pleasure as a conductor. He was a profound artist. What an experience to listen to Bach's *Brandenburg* Concerto no. 5 with Furtwängler playing the piano! He had a broad view of the whole, and his personality had the mysterious knack of establishing a magnetic contact with both audience and orchestra alike without resorting to histrionics. It is a very rare gift. Many artists with wide musical knowledge do not have the projection to carry their performances across the footlights. I found Erich Kleiber an excellent conductor, but thoroughly uninspiring. Nor did I find Klemperer at that time to my liking. On the other hand, in Bruno Walter I found an artist of great poetry and I listened to him with pleasure.

I had heard Stokowski many times when he was conducting the Philadelphia Orchestra at the height of his career. I was young and impressed by his personality, his virtuoso craftsmanship which enabled him to obtain the most ravishing effects from an orchestra. Eventually I met him on a ship crossing the Atlantic from New York to Italy. The length of the journey – eight days at that time – and the very few passengers on board (it was a mid-winter trip) gave us the opportunity to spend long hours together, and to strike up a lasting acquaintance. He was very concerned with maintaining his incognito, and he had put himself on the passenger list under an assumed name. Unfortunately an electric-blue suit, matching suede shoes, a pink shirt and harmonising socks, canary-yellow gloves and outsize pair of dark glasses under the famous blond mane of the Maestro, proclaimed his presence to reporters, photographers and passengers alike.

I knew Stokowski musically long before I met him personally, through his famous recordings of the Bach Toccata and Fugue in D Minor, Schubert's *Unfinished* Symphony, and many others no less spectacular. I was amazed by the perfection of his Philadelphia Orchestra, and by the lush sound he could produce. But music is not just a pretty noise. In my opinion his conducting conveyed pleasure to the ear alone, accompanied by a beautiful choreographic display of movements. However, his musical leadership was superb, commanding the orchestra's total allegiance. He had an admirably proportioned figure, a handsome profile (although a rather large nose), and a small sensual mouth with a drooping lower lip. He appeared simple and sweet, and yet one had the feeling that underneath there was something false. His speech was particularly affected; his fictitious accent and mannerisms cultivated over the years became second nature to him. He gave the impression of a glittering, multi-coloured, painted shell; when one looked inside one found an infinite emptiness.

He sometimes took a vicious pleasure in upsetting people. During our crossing together he insisted on attending a concert put on by the ship's orchestra. I tried to dissuade him, pointing out that musicians on board are not always the best, and that it might be embarrassing to them and unpleasant for us. He ignored my advice, and half an hour before the concert began he was sitting in the front row ostentatiously waiting for the performers to appear.

What happened later was sad and unkind. A Beethoven trio was the first number on the programme and the three performers, already informed of Stokowski's presence, were clearly suffering from nervous strain. The performance left much to be desired. Stokowski, frowning at every wrong note, showed signs of disapproval and then left in the middle of the first movement.

Someone told me that after Toscanini's first triumphant concert in London after the war, an admirer said jokingly to the Maestro, 'I know of a conductor in the audience tonight who committed suicide!' Toscanini found this perfectly natural and remarked, 'Oh really, what's his name?' An artist is easily convinced that mankind cannot manage without him.

Similarly, I recall an evening spent at Toscanini's house in Riverdale a few years before his death. He was in an unusually good mood. We sat alone in the drawing-room, and the Maestro was reminiscing about his long life, his devotion to music, and his dedication to his art. He spoke with wisdom and serenity advising me to be humble, to be modest. 'Our life is a priest-

Toscanini at Verdi's funeral, awaiting the arrival of the coffin: Milan, 26 February 1900.

hood, and modesty is the most important factor.' He then got up and, pointing his forefinger at his chest, added imperiously: 'And I, I, *I*, Toscanini, tell you this!'

During the period I spent as musical director and conductor of the New Orleans Symphony Orchestra, and later of the Baltimore Symphony Orchestra, whenever I could squeeze two or three days out of my busy schedule my wife and I would rush to New York to see the Maestro and hear one of his concerts. We also spoke regularly on the telephone, especially after his Sunday concerts with NBC; he would ring me to inquire about the quality of the broadcasts.

My reserve and shyness, not to mention his forbidding personality, prevented me from asking his advice about music, but he could somehow charge you with his energy and dynamism. A few hours with 'the old man' was an exhilarating experience. His power of mastering scores, his devotion to music, his austerity and his immense effort to project the most accurate version of the composer's concept impressed not only people in his immediate circle but the whole musical world.

Toscanini set an absolute standard of integrity influencing musical interpretations: he was the embodiment of the artistic conscience. If he were alive now there would be fewer displays of shallow exhibitionism. I have seen great interpreters such as Horowitz and Heifetz nervous in front of the Maestro, not daring to indulge in mannerisms or *rubati* not quite in keeping with the composer's intentions. He would never have allowed the stage director to take advantage of the music in order to gain a visual effect and himself taught the singers how to act, always in accordance with the demands of the music. In 1921 he engaged a stage director, Gioacchino Forzano, at La Scala for the first time. He insisted that action and movement should emphasise the impact of the drama, but above all that the music should always be the prime concern.

Toscanini's sense of rhythm and balance was unique. His control of an *accellerando* or *ritardando* was as geometrically perfect as the enlarging or shrinking of the beam of a reflector. His beat conveyed such a steady flow that each voice of the orchestral score moved smoothly as if on a separate track, allowing each player to perform at his best, and consequently obtain an extraordinary clarity. This crystalline purity helped his gifted ear to detect the slightest imperfection and to unite the various sounds of the orchestra in perfect harmony.

His rehearsals were an unforgettable experience. Half an hour before they started, the members of the orchestra were already in the grip of an extraordinary tension. Oboes nervously testing the best reed, violins brushing up the most difficult passages, brasses carefully checking the intonation, a rising excitement culminating in dead silence when the little man entered from the wings.

Now Toscanini was on the podium to give life to his interpretation. In spite of his magnetic power and the limitless dedication of the players, it was a ferocious struggle. Most of the time his dissatisfaction at not being able to reach the summit of his conception, to conquer the unattainable, to embody the intent of the composer, drove him to fury and his orchestra to despair. His search for the ultimate truth and his supreme idealism could not conceive of an imperfect realisation. I recall at a recording session of Strauss's *Death and Transfiguration* that the Maestro, who had just conducted it in public the night before, flew into a rage as soon as the muted violins began: they had not played half of the first bar when a deluge of abuse fell on them – the rhythm was wrong, the *pianissimi* were too loud, the balance was incorrect. He goaded the men into such a frenzy for about twenty minutes that when he reached the third bar the wind instruments were incapable of playing the C minor chord. That recording session was cancelled, but a sublime performance of *Death and Transfiguration* was recorded a few days later.

Many books have touched on the Maestro's strict observance of the score. This is fallacious. There are numerous changes in his orchestral parts. In Beethoven's Ninth Symphony the modifications in the first, second and last movements reveal his obsession with the best realisation of the composer's meaning. In Debussy's *La Mer* the last bars of the first movement are completely retouched in order to enrich the brightness of 'De l'aube à midi sur la mer'. He could not admit that an interpretative message could be carried through by an imperfectly orchestrated score.

I have always thought that Toscanini's artistic expression sprang from forces having little to do with music in our general sense. His interpretative genius burst forth when dealing with highly emotional feelings or cosmic elements – fire, water, cataclysms of nature. His magic wand unchained the wrath of God in Verdi's 'Dies Irae', the storm in Beethoven's *Pastoral* Symphony and the 'Dialogue of the Wind and the Sea' in Debussy's *La Mer*. Toscanini was seldom happy. I was shocked when he told me once, at the height of his career, 'I have never had a happy day in my life.' I think it was true. He was often displeased with himself. He was always upset by a person's lack of integrity and by an artist indulging in vulgar effects, or not adhering to the composer's intentions. I believe Toscanini's interpretative powers derived not only from intellectual reasoning but from the dramatic emotion tempered by a balanced Latin mind. My wife asked him once in my presence which composer he preferred, Haydn or Mozart. 'Haydn,' he replied, 'there is blood in Haydn.' He then sprang from his chair and fetched the score of Mozart's *Requiem* which was lying on the piano. 'Look, look,' he almost shouted, 'in the "Tuba Mirum" he scores only *one* trombone'; and he threw the book on the floor in distress. With Toscanini's sense of drama it was inconceivable that words such as 'Tuba mirum spargens / Per sepulchra regionum / Coget omnes ante thronum'* should be so thinly scored.

If Toscanini looked fierce and unapproachable, there was a touching human side to his nature. One evening I drove with him to Riverdale. After dinner he asked me to follow him to his

*'The last loud trumpet's spreading tone / Shall through the place of tombs be blown / To summon all before the throne.'

148

MF and Toscanini, Torcello, 1949.

studio as he wanted to hear the news about the war in Europe. It was 14 November 1944, the day that Milan was bombed and La Scala partly destroyed. The Maestro burst into tears. Then he took my hand and told me about his conflict with the Fascists, including the incident in Bologna on 14 May 1931. He was to conduct a memorial concert there for Giuseppe Martucci, in which only works of this composer would be performed. After the general rehearsal he was asked if he would play the Fascist song 'Giovinezza' at the concert that evening as some Fascist officials were going to be present. Toscanini replied that it did not seem appropriate, considering the nature of the concert. Despite several telephone calls advising him to change his mind, he persisted in his refusal. That evening on arrival at the Teatro Communale accompanied by his wife Carla and his daughter

Wanda, he was met by a group of Fascist hoodlums who attacked him. He was severely beaten and only saved by the prompt action of his Swiss chauffeur, Emilio.

If he was violent with the orchestra he was never vicious. Whatever he believed he stated without fear or diplomacy, not only about music but also about politics. He was courageous and generous. When Hitler marched into Austria he cancelled his engagements in Salzburg and went to conduct for the Jews in Tel-Aviv in order to help them organise an orchestra, without remuneration for himself. He supported people in need – he donated generously to the Casa Verdi for retired musicians, and there were many other instances of his munificence that were never revealed.

He has often been criticised for not helping the young and for not performing enough modern music. In his youth, while he was conductor at La Scala, he introduced to Italy Debussy's *Pelléas and Melisande*, Strauss's *Salome,* premières of operas by Puccini and Mascagni, as well as a host of operas by minor composers. In the programme of symphony concerts there was always a modern piece by Malipiero, De Sabata, Sinigaglia, Tommasini and many others. While touring in Europe with the New York Philharmonic, he conducted music by Pizzetti, *Concerto dell' Estate* and *Rondò Veneziano,* in most of his concerts, although his music never had any success with the press or the public.

Toscanini had an intellectual curiosity and a desire to understand modern composers. I remember once, after having had luncheon with the Maestro in Riverdale, accompanying him to the RCA Studio 8H to listen to a rehearsal of Alban Berg's violin concerto – Dimitri Mitropoulos was conducting and Joseph Szigeti was the soloist. We sat in a box right on the stage. During the rehearsal the Maestro, who seemed keenly interested in the music, asked me to bring him an extra score from the library. Towards the end, after showing signs of restlessness, he suddenly stood up, flung down the score and muttered 'I understand the

MF and Luigi Dallapiccola, Connecticut.

Ninth Symphony, why can't I understand *this* music?' He left and I followed him towards the entrance where Signora Toscanini was waiting. We were in the car when the Maestro asked again for Alban Berg's score – 'I must, I must study that score tonight, I must understand that music.' It was the same determination to learn that had him, in his late middle age, studying Shakespeare like a young student. He would write down archaic phrases which he would then translate into Italian for his own information.

When Dallapiccola was teaching in Tanglewood, I invited him to be the soloist in his own piano concerto at one of my concerts with the NBC Orchestra. Toscanini, who had been in Italy, returned unexpectedly to New York. I confess I was uneasy as I knew Dallapiccola's music was not particularly to his taste. He called me on the telephone and said 'I know you have engaged as soloist in one of your concerts with my orchestra one of your old Conservatory friends.' At the end of our conversation he told me how right I was to perform music of my own generation and how much modern music he had conducted in his youth. He invited my wife and myself to dine after the concert and asked me to bring my 'vecchio compagno del conservatorio' as well. Although he limited himself to expressing his appreciation of my performance he did not say a word to Dallapiccola about his music. At first the atmosphere was a little strained, but Dallapiccola's brilliant dialectics soon won over the Maestro. There followed a masterful thank-you letter from Dallapiccola to Toscanini, a cordial reply from Toscanini to Dallapiccola, and a moving letter from Dallapiccola to me, grateful for the opportunity I had given him of meeting the Maestro.

Having just finished my engagements with the Baltimore Symphony Orchestra, my wife and I went to New York to hear the Maestro's closing concert of the season, on Sunday 4 April 1954. We arrived the day before the general rehearsal; the programme was an all-Wagner one, with all his 'war horses'. He began with the first act prelude to *Lohengrin*, which went smoothly, as did the *Forest Murmurs*, the second piece in the programme. In *Siegfried's* 'Rhine Journey' he had an argument with the tympanist about an entrance. Toscanini lost his temper and began shouting all sorts of insults at the entire orchestra: 'For seventeen years I have tried to teach you how to play and you have never learnt, I am ashamed of you.' He then threw down his baton and left the stage. We all thought he would continue to rehearse after quietening down (it had happened on other occasions) but eventually the orchestra was dismissed. A feeling of gloom came over the few people present in Carnegie Hall. We all believed the following day's performance would be cancelled, but an announcement later informed us that Toscanini would conduct the concert after all. We left deeply disturbed, and I was haunted by a presentiment. The Maestro was not himself. I had never seen him give in before, I was frightened. I did not want to attend that concert.

On the day, the customary ovation greeted him when he appeared from the wings, but he barely nodded to the audience, turning to the orchestra and abruptly starting the prelude to *Lohengrin*. He appeared distracted: his eyes, under the bushy eyebrows, lacked their usual fire and his powerful jaw the determined set so typical of the Maestro. He looked defeated. His famous beat was unclear; he just stared at the floor as if his mind were elsewhere. The members of the orchestra felt increasingly insecure. As the uneasiness spread, some leaders attempted to guide their own sections in order to avoid a catastrophe.

In *Tannhäuser's* 'Venusberg Music' there was real panic when the orchestra became completely lost. The Maestro's protégé, Guido Cantelli, rushed backstage to discontinue the broadcast, playing instead Toscanini's recording of Brahms's First Symphony while the concert itself went on. Toscanini did not seem to hear what was happening. He leant on the rail at the back of the rostrum, his left hand clutching a handkerchief with which he occasionally wiped his forehead. The *Meistersinger* Overture was the concert's closing item. The Maestro let the orchestra play alone, he did not move. Towards the end he let fall his baton and walked slowly off the stage. He never conducted in public again.

The following day his daughter Wally telephoned me to ask my wife and myself if we would lunch with her father in an Italian restaurant in New Jersey, just across the bridge and not far from Riverdale. Toscanini was silent and depressed. I was sitting next to him and noticed that he had difficulty in handling his knife and fork, and in reaching for his bread or his glass.

Towards the end of the meal he gave me a heartbroken look. 'You know, I did not conduct well yesterday,' he said quietly. But he intended to conduct in Salzburg during the summer. As I had been asked to change the conversation if he touched on the subject of future concerts, I switched the topic to Berlioz's *Damnation of Faust*, a work that I was about to conduct in the near future and that would remind the Maestro of his long-past performances at La Scala. His mood changed abruptly. He spoke with animation and lucidity of the singers – of a very stupid bass, who having no talent for acting was the perfect Brander, standing centre-stage with a mug in his hands during the tavern scene.

Although 4 April 1954 was his last public appearance, a few months later, as he was dissatisfied with some parts of *Aïda* which he had previously recorded, RCA assembled the orchestra to repeat two arias with the soprano Herva Nelli – 'Ritorna Vincitor' and 'O Patria Mia'.

The Maestro was tired. He went to Italy for a rest and spent some time at his beloved Isolino on the Lago Maggiore. The next years were divided between Riverdale and Milan, and I saw him frequently in both places.

During the last months of his life he spent much time listening to old tapes which had not been released by the recording company. He once played me an orchestral excerpt from Dukas's *Arianne et Barbe-bleu*, as well as part of Berlioz's *Damnation of Faust*, Roussel's *Festin de l'Araignée* and other performances of many years past, copies of which he gave me as a present.

On 1 January 1957 Maestro suffered a stroke, after which he remained unconscious for fifteen days. He died on 16 January. After his death I asked his son Walter, 'Did Maestro sometimes recognise people?' 'Oh no,' he replied, 'but in his coma he repeated: 'Guerra ... Guerra ... Guerra ... Guerra ... Guerra.' He was still rehearsing *Aïda* – the scene of the priests declaring war on Ethiopia. Even on his deathbed he did not want to surrender. In his subconscious he was fighting the last battle.

Toscanini has been dead for some years, and I often think of the influence he has had on my life and my work. In me he strengthened the concept of morality in music, and the need to approach it with a priestly humility and love. He increased

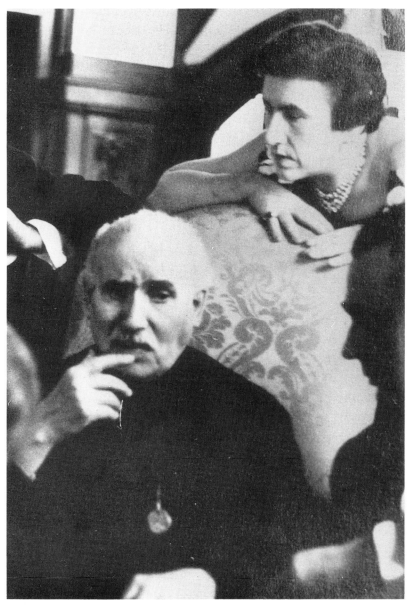

Last photograph of Toscanini (with daughter Wanda), New Year's Eve, 1956.

my desire to search out and meditate on the deepest interpretative questions: the meaning of dynamics as suggestions and not as ultimate conclusions, and above all, the unravelling of the composer's wishes unfettered by established concepts and tradition.

Toscanini often talked to me at length about Puccini, whom he loved and admired. They were the closest of friends for many, many years, and very often Puccini would come to Toscanini's house to play his latest compositions at the piano. 'Once he brought me a sketch of *Bohème*'s first act,' Toscanini said, frowning, then continued, 'and played me the tenor's aria, "Ai cieli bigi guardo fumar da mille comignoli di Parigi". I told him, "Giacomo, the rhythm is wrong, the prosody is incorrect, you must work on this aria." But he was lazy, he let it pass ... and it is still wrong.' A veil of sadness covered his myopic eyes. 'With his talent he could have done better in *Butterfly*. Just before "Un bel dì vedremo", I told him "Giacomo, look, *look* how Wagner gradually builds up to a dramatic moment – and what do you do? ... You've scored a long *diminuendo*." But he was *un facilone* [easy going], longing to go coot shooting at the Lago di Massaciuccoli, or chasing girls.' Toscanini spoke in his usual hoarse voice, sometimes with profound unhappiness, occasionally raising his tone as if he were reliving that moment and still able to advise his friend.

This intimate friendship with Puccini was ruptured when Toscanini was rehearsing *Nerone* by Boito at the Scala, and he had given strict orders not to let anyone in at the general rehearsal. When Puccini was forbidden to enter the theatre he was deeply offended. For a long time they did not speak. It was in Turin, while Toscanini was conducting there, that Gioacchino Forzano, the stage director, told him that Puccini was seriously ill at his home in Tuscany, Torre del Lago, and that he was about to leave for an operation in Brussels. There were doubts whether

Photograph of Puccini, inscribed to MF's mother, 1897.

he would survive. Toscanini immediately left with his daughter Wanda to visit him. It was a very moving reunion. They spent long hours at the piano playing his unfinished opera *Turandot*. Puccini, who was suffering from cancer of the throat, sang the different parts as best he could. At the end he said, smiling, 'Sono diventato un tenorino' – 'I have become a little tenor.'

He died shortly afterwards. His final resting-place at Torre del Lago was still unfinished. Until that time the body lay in the Toscanini family tomb in Milan.

I recall how once in my youth, longing to attend a general re-hearsal of a Puccini opera, I fooled the porter by sneaking in carrying an empty violin case, wearing a slouch hat and a pair of dark glasses to disguise my age. After gaining entry, I abandoned the violin case in a dark corridor and headed for the stalls. All the chairs except for three at the back (one already occupied by an elderly gentleman resting both hands on his walking stick) were covered with heavy dust sheets. There was no one else present. His paternal look inspired confidence and I sat next to him feeling that he would protect me. The performance of *Tosca* unfolded; during the long intervals the dim lighting in the hall gave my companion ample time for a placid doze. When the music resumed, he once again listened attentively.

It was at the beginning of the third act that I wished I had never embarked on this venture. All of a sudden my companion got up, banging his cane and shouting in fury: 'The bells! The bells! Who are those idiots playing the bells?' In anguish I tried to grab him by his coat-tails, whispering that he must not make such a noise and that we would both be thrown out. Deaf to my warnings, he kept on yelling until the rehearsal was brought to a halt. A throng of people came running in our direction and crowded round my seat next to the aisle. My escape blocked, I sat timorously in my place, trying to make myself as unobtrusive as possible. The man sitting next to me was Giacomo Puccini.

After recovering his self-control he proceeded to explain how the bells should be played, the type of mallets to be used on them and how far away they should be placed in order to obtain the right effect. The beginning of the third act was repeated several times until the proper balance was attained. Many years later I myself conducted *Tosca*. I was particularly concerned to apply the teaching of the composer.

When I was told that Herbert von Karajan had died, I said that I was shocked, that it was a terrible loss. Truthfully I was not as upset as I sounded; though I could only admire Karajan's gifts, I did not like him as a man. As a musician I believe he was the last of the generation of real conductors, like Toscanini, Furtwängler and Bruno Walter. He started his career in small provincial cities, building up his natural talents and developing his superb musicianship until he had an impressive international reputation. His memory was exceptional. He conducted by heart operas and scores of the most diverse styles, from Wagner, Verdi, Debussy and Puccini to Schoenberg, but always with the same rounded mellow tone from the orchestra. This, for him, was of primary importance, regardless of the character of the composition. I think that as a conductor he will be remembered for his achievement in creating a recording empire and for his beautiful 'Karajan sound', rather than for a legitimate or profound interpretation of the major composers.

I first met Karajan in the United States when he was touring with the Berlin Philharmonic Orchestra. On the day he was conducting in Baltimore I had gone to New York to hear Toscanini performing Beethoven's *Missa Solemnis*. On my return late that evening the telephone was ringing. It was Raffaele Canevaro, the Italian consul-general in that city, to tell me that Karajan was at his house and very much wanted to meet me as he was a great friend of my brother. An intimate supper was ready and they were anxious for us to join them.

I found Karajan charming. He made you think that you were the only person in the world who mattered to him. The admiration he had for my brother was boundless – he called him the most intelligent man he had ever met. He also told me how much he appreciated all that my brother had done to help him after the war during the period when he was not allowed to conduct. (When my brother died, knowing how intimate he and Karajan had been, I wrote him a letter. He never answered.) His secretary, André von Mattoni, an ex-actor and a professional charmer, underlined every compliment with his own captivating remarks. We talked at length about music, and about the recent offer Karajan had received to become life conductor of the Berlin Philarmonic, which he still felt doubtful about accepting. I was to conduct his orchestra, the Wiener Synphoniker, in the Festwoche that spring, and he told me that a warm welcome was awaiting me.

I saw him on many occasions after that, mostly in Europe. He was a good-looking man; his eyes in repose were gentle and warm, but they could change suddenly to become as hard as steel. His most obvious characteristic, I suppose, was his ruthlessness: he would hesitate at nothing to get what he wanted. He could detach himself from his work at the flick of a switch. The last time I saw him it was at an all-Brahms concert which he was conducting in the Musikverein. He had asked me to go and see him in the interval. I sat with him while he had a meeting with several managers to organise a tour with the orchestra. He was abruptly stopped in order to resume the concert, invited me to have supper with him, walked straight to the podium and started Brahms's Fourth Symphony. It was a beautiful performance.

It is a mistake to generalise about the Italians. In that part of Tuscany from the hill of Fiesole through the valley of Florence, up to the foot of the Pisan mountains in the north and Siena in the west, a race settled which had little resemblance to the other inhabitants of the peninsula. After a millennium their physical characteristics have undergone little change. They retain a fair complexion, a bony physiognomy, and a mind served by a brisk intelligence. Instinctively, Tuscans are not warriors or conquerors; their passions are often calculating and mean, they tend to faction, but they have a mysterious spirituality which is intellectual rather than emotional. In my opinion, that which governs a Tuscan is a natural philosophy of being and knowing, manifest in the purity of all forms of expression. Their architecture, in contrast to the Roman, is austere, their palaces forbidding, their religion free from picturesque images of saints. For them it is mysticism that is the basis of religion. If wealth and prosperity usually bring power and consequently pomposity and self-indulgence in their wake, in Florence they have produced progress, artistic achievement and freedom of the individual. The rebellious character of the Tuscan is the result of his concept of liberty; that is to say, he is unimpressed by ostentation and formality. From the plain artisan to the great names of the Florentine aristocracy and the many geniuses who have given so much to the world's culture, there is one affinity – simplicity. I often feel a nostalgia for Tuscany, but there is no longer any question of my returning to live in Florence itself. I have been self-exiled too long, too many friends and relatives have disappeared, and, above all, too many changes have taken place since the day I left it. But I will always have the feeling that my natural centre lies there.

I now look back only to remember the rewarding moments of the many years when I was conductor of the RAI Orchestra. Among the concerts I conducted, the two given for Pope John XXIII will remain deeply impressed on my mind. I had the good fortune to perform in the Sala delle Benedizioni in the Basilica di S. Pietro, at a time when the splendour of papal magnificence still existed. The Pope was escorted by the Guardia Nobile to a throne on the left of a platform built specially for the orchestra, where he sat surrounded by his immediate court. The College of Cardinals, in their bright red robes, occupied the front row, behind them came ranks of archbishops, bishops and monsignori in purple vestments, and to the rear the various orders of monks. The diplomatic corps were formally dressed in tailcoat, white tie and decorations, with the traditional black waistcoat, worn in the papal presence. Behind them, admitted by invitation, were the public. It was a majestic sight, a spectacle arranged down to the minutest detail by the highly efficient office of the Vatican's protocol, which left nothing to chance. Unfortunately, at one of my concerts the unexpected happened.

The occasion was televised, in particular to countries beyond the Iron Curtain, and extra time had been assigned to the announcer for translation into various languages. Every movement was planned and timed to a split second.

The performance was scheduled for half past six. I was supposed to step onto the podium at 6.29 to await His Holiness, who on entering the hall had the exact time to reach the throne and give the order for the concert to begin, after the usual blessing. I was in my dressing-room, built for the occasion – a sort of baldachin in rich red silk damask, furnished with a gilded armchair and a cushion of the same material as a foot-rest – when at twenty-five past six a panting monsignor burst under my canopy to announce that His Holiness would enter the Sala in a few moments. I rushed to the stage and stepped onto the podium at the precise moment when the Pope was making his entrance to the hall. The orchestra stood up, the audience knelt down, and in a respectful silence one could hear only the smooth swift swishing of the satin gowns of the papal retinue walking towards the throne. In a matter of seconds everyone was re-seated, and a paternal gesture from His Holiness gave me the order to begin the concert. It was not yet half past six, and the concealed little light which, when green, would have given me the signal to start the performance, was inexorably switched off. I could see the producer, tele-technicians and others in a state of great excitement, making separate gestures to hold on, as we were not yet on the air and the announcement in three different languages had still to be read. In order to kill time, I pulled my right cuff, then the left; I straightened my white tie, always keeping an anxious eye on the warning light to see if it were flashing. While the Pope renewed his order to begin, a television producer on all fours in the trombone section was begging me to wait, with frantic gesticulations. Before starting a concert, some conductors keep their eyes closed in concentration or give a Napoleonic look to galvanise their men; pianists always wind their stool to adjust its height, violinists pluck the strings or twitch the pad on their left shoulder; but I thought that in a holy place it might be appropriate to kill time by assuming a mystic air, looking at the ceiling as if I were waiting for divine inspiration. I could see out of the corner of my left eye His Holiness inquiring from his *segretario di camera* the reason for the delay. In a typical Italian gesture he was shaking his upturned right hand, fingers joined together with the thumb. It was an enormous relief when the green light rescued me from four minutes which had seemed an eternity.

Since Pope John XXIII democratised the Church, the pomp and beauty have vanished; Pope Paul VI abolished the colourful Guardia Nobile, the cardinals' red satin trains have been docked for economy, monsignori no longer dress in purple, nuns have abandoned their medieval costumes to look more and more like airline stewardesses, and the annual Vatican performance is given in a regular concert hall where the Pope sits in the front row like anyone else. I wonder if the external appeal of the seat of Peter is not universally diminished by drastic reforms: to abandon the pageantry and to slacken the strict rules which controlled its ritual worldwide may eventually give Roman Catholicism the appearance of a dry, colourless Puritan sect.

(Overleaf) Vatican concert, April 1960.

Tradition is the fruit of past experience, and the unchanging rites of the Church of Rome keep the torch of Christendom burning over the Seven Hills.

The beauty and the mild climate of the Italian Riviera had lured my brother into spending a year away from the city whilst recovering from a lung ailment. He had moved into a converted farmhouse on a slope between Santa Margherita and Rapallo. One of those foreigners who think of Italy as an ideal place for retirement had made an enchanting home out of a modest rustic building. The structure was odd. A large living-room on the ground floor formed the main part of the house. Built for maximum height, it merged the stable with the hay-loft above; a huge oak beam which once supported the rafters had been kept as a decoration. The bedrooms, on account of the steeply sloping terrain, were all constructed on different levels connected by steps and passages, which gave a certain charm to an otherwise confusing labyrinth. There was no garden, but only olive trees – to one of which Oreste was permanently tied. Oreste was an old Sardinian donkey whose function it was to carry provisions over the precipitous muletrack from the main road to the house. The view was stupendous. From Portofino's point, stretching to Levanto on the left, the white and pink houses dotting the green slope of the valley seemed like a garland tossed into the sea.

My brother and I, although brought up together from infancy until the time I left my father's house to go and live in Vienna, never had a great affinity – indeed I would say that we were almost unfriendly. His interests were painting and science and he chose his friends from a world different from mine. His liking for a disorderly Bohemian life, which grieved my conventional father, also irked me. Born when my mother was frail and in poor health, he had inherited a hypersensitive physique which could at any moment develop a psychosomatic illness. Spoilt by my parents in his childhood and by his admirers all his life, he

Vieri painting, 1949.

was whimsical, irresponsible, and given to moods of depression and elation. Endowed with many natural gifts, he was always surrounded by a group of acolytes – both men and women – captivated by his brilliant intelligence and his poetic and empirical theories. He was a fluent talker, and from his early youth friends would converge on his studio to listen to his imaginative speculations on art, science, mathematics or politics. Physically he was handsome: fair, tall, with a classic Florentine profile, and an expressive and engaging look that was his essential charm. He had a drooping left eyelid and a smile that had an irresistible effect on women. When still very young, he devoted himself to painting. His technique was remarkable. As an artist he always remained representational, yet there was such a spiritual expression in his portraits that his style, although academic, was never dated. He was at home with technology and he was an inventor. However, his profusion of gifts caused him to squander his time in too many ways. If one considers his talents he was a failure, but he made his masterpiece out of life itself. His merciless wit, his wide knowledge, his radical reaction to conventionalism, his odd amorality made him a fascinating personality.

I admired him, but his unjustifiable cruelty towards our father prejudiced me against him. After several years of separation we were reunited at my father's funeral. I recall returning from the cemetery; we spent hours looking back on things past, on our childhood. He spoke with such clarity of 'the *a priori* elements in his youthful experiences', as he called them, that through this transcendental imagery we were reconciled to each other. He had a lyrical gift. Too weak to face reality, he wandered in the realms of fantasy with such assurance that his listeners would follow spellbound. Despite his many gifts, subconsciously he never wanted achievement. He never determined his path through life; he preferred to remain changeable and inconclusive. He retained friendship if he was unconditionally admired. I think he had a deep affection for me, although he resented my orderly life and was sarcastic about my bourgeois devotion not only to music but to only one wife. Strangely enough, even with his Bohemian character, he always had a conventional desire to give his love affairs legality and to procreate. There was nothing of the frivolous lover in him; he was a dedicated polygamist, with many homes and many children.

On account of his physical weakness he seldom left the house. Occasionally, on very hot days we sat outdoors. We talked for hours while he worked at a self-portrait, and I appreciated his conversation; whatever topic he discussed, he was original, and

Vieri Freccia, self-portrait.

when in a good mood a marvellous companion. However, his moods of depression were so unpleasant that we all spoilt him in humouring his sudden fancies.

Towards the end of his life my brother edited a book about Naples, a superb folio edition of prints and maps. While he was working on it, he stayed with an old friend of mine, Paolo Gaetani, in his villa in Torre del Greco, under the shadow of Mount Vesuvius. When I was in Naples to conduct a concert at the Teatro San Carlo, Paolo Gaetani telephoned to ask my wife and myself over to lunch. It was good to see him again. We spoke about my brother and the book, and he told me a curious tailpiece to its publication.

In August 1962 Jacqueline Kennedy had been a guest on the Agnelli yacht in the Mediterranean, and her host rang to ask if the party might pay a visit to the Gaetanis at Torre del Greco. The hospitable Paolo and his wife Edna laid on what must have been a magical evening, with hundreds of Roman torches lighting the terraces of the villa garden. After dinner the guests were taken to see the moonlit view of Vesuvius from the study window. There was a print in Vieri's book of Vesuvius erupting, and Paolo Gaetani took his copy from its library shelf to show it to Mrs Kennedy. Now, I have no Secret Service training but it would surprise me if browsing in one's host's library constitutes a high-risk activity – unless he happens to be unusually possessive about his books, and no one could have been more open-handed than Paolo Gaetani. So when a bullet suddenly sang past the First Lady and lodged itself in the library wall, the effect on the entourage can be imagined. There were Secret Service men everywhere, blocking the escape routes, climbing through the windows, checking the roof.

The explanation was innocent, if not exactly music to a security man's ear. A loaded pistol had been unwisely left on a desk in the study and a journalist had accidentally pulled the trigger. Mrs Kennedy behaved as if nothing had happened, continuing to examine the book with such obvious enthusiasm that Paolo Gaetani asked her to accept it as a gift. I saw the letter she wrote in thanks the following day, charm itself, written in French. Of the dinner – 'Lucullus n'avait jamais dîné comme ça'; of the book and the incident – Comme souvenir j'ai ce merveilleux livre de gravures de Naples qui est mon plus grand trésor, et vous avez une balle dans le mur de votre bibliothèque.'

In April 1953 we were crossing from New York to Europe on the *Queen Elizabeth*. His Imperial Highness Prince Akihito was on board with his retinue on his way to England to attend the Coronation.

The second day at sea, the purser, Lionel Carine, came to our cabin to inform us that the Prince wanted to meet a few of the passengers, and that my wife and I were amongst the small group selected by H.I.H. for a cocktail party the following day. My wife, accepting enthusiastically, announced that she spoke Japanese. She had been in Japan for two months in 1935.

The whole thing was organised with a strict royal protocol. The Commodore, standing beside the Prince in the centre of the room, introduced the guests amid much curtsying and bowing; then attentive stewards escorted them to their tables. It was not, at the beginning, one of the most animated parties I have ever attended. The Prince, accompanied by his equerries and the Commodore, paid a special visit to each table, but the guests were having an agonising time searching for a word to say. Although heartened by an artificial smile from the equerries, they were immediately discouraged by the Prince's stony look.

Eventually H.I.H. sat at our table. We had with us Lily Pons and an American couple from Philadelphia. The Commodore turned to my wife and told her that he had heard from Carine that she spoke Japanese. This she confirmed with a smile, adding that she could also sing 'The Tokiondo' – a very popular song in

On the Queen Elizabeth, *1956*.

Japan in 1935. H.I.H. did not know the song – it was a shade before his time – but his equerries appeared greatly excited. The Prince asked my wife if she would sing it, and his retinue volunteered to join the chorus, which as far as I remember consisted of two words, 'Yoi, yoi'. The success was clamorous. The Prince's face broke into a smile, the ice was broken and the Commodore looked extremely relieved.

Leopold Stokowski, sitting at another table with his wife Gloria Vanderbilt, and a bit annoyed at not being the centre of attraction, came to our table and asked the son of the Emperor if he could give him some information on the music in the ancient imperial Court of Japan. H.I.H., whose rigid tenure had progressively loosened up, burst into a laugh and said, 'I don't know. Ask Mrs Freccia.'

We left the ship at Cherbourg as we were travelling to Paris. When we descended the gangplank, we turned to wave to

Carine. Prince Akihito and his equerries were all bowing deeply to my wife in a perfectly synchronised movement.

I encountered this enigmatic element in the Japanese when I went to conduct in Japan in 1967. At my first rehearsal, the day after our arrival in Tokyo, I had the pleasure of working with one of the best orchestras I have ever conducted in my life, the NHK – Nippon Hoso Kyokai. I confess that I was previously rather prejudiced, as I had heard the orchestra while they were on tour in Europe, and although I appreciated their superb precision, I found their performance somewhat mechanical and lacking in emotional depth. Furthermore, I remembered a story told to me by Paul Kletzki after he returned from conducting a Japanese orchestra. Kletzki, an excellent conductor with a personality inclined towards compassionate Polish-Jewish emotion, was perturbed while rehearsing a Brahms symphony by the detached approach of the orchestra. He abruptly stopped the players and said, 'Gentlemen, do you like music?' The whole orchestra rose, bowing deeply and inhaling noisily through their teeth. 'Gentlemen, do you like Brahms?' Another approving bow, with the same assenting sound. 'In our Western world, when we make music we participate not only with our hearts, but also with our bodies. We swing, we move, we show our enthusiasm.' He regretted having said this. The night of the concert, the entire string section swayed to and fro so violently that he was almost seasick. Personally I did not find the orchestra indifferent, nor alien to our emotions. We had a Tchaikovsky symphony in the first programme which was played with deep feeling and a rich sound from the strings. Yet from the moment I landed in Tokyo I had the impression that the principal desire of the Japanese was 'to please in every way'.

Once at a rehearsal a soloist in the woodwind section of the orchestra made a trivial mistake. It was not due to incompetence or lack of attention, but merely a rhythmic misunderstanding, which was duly corrected after I had hummed the part. The poor fellow, embarrassed and humiliated in front of his colleagues, kept on bowing deeply, asking for forgiveness. It reminded me of an occasion when a noted European conductor reprimanded a player. The dishonour was such that not only was the man discharged, but the chief of personnel responsible for his engagement felt it his duty to give his spiritual and material support to the player and his family, since they had fallen into irretrievable disgrace. Japan is the opposite of Italy, where nobody suffers from a guilt complex: the Italians can unburden themselves in the confessional. The Japanese see sin differently. To be caught erring, especially in front of a Westerner, is the unforgivable.

I had just returned from a trip to Japan when I received a message from my brother asking me to call him at his house in Milan. I finally got in touch with him and he told me calmly that he had only a few months to live. He was taking advantage of an invitation from a friend who had a house near the sea to go fishing.

When I saw him a few days later it was by the shores of the Mediterranean. He was pale, drawn and serene, and spoke of death with indifference, with an intense meditative look in his eyes. We walked to the harbour. He untied a small boat from its mooring, started the engine, and we set out to sea. I sat on the edge of the cockpit while he searched in a rusty tin box for hooks, unknotting a line, keeping his forearm over the tiller. He was the first to break the long silence.

'I am a realist. I don't believe in God. I now start my solitary trip to the uninhabited.' He paused for a long time, staring at the horizon, then he continued: 'I cannot conceive of an existence without a body, but soon my body will cease to exist, and I only hope that there is a spiritual force in the universe to justify our sufferings, our loves and our passions.'

Three months later he died in a clinic in Milan. A Dominican nun who took care of the ward told me, 'This morning at six he asked for a priest, he confessed, took Communion and received Extreme Unction.' At the end of his human life, before the dissolution of consciousness, he regained his faith and through the Church entered into the spiritual universe for which he had hoped.

With his death I was suddenly confronted by the fact that an earthly life which had run its course parallel with my own had reached its end, and that something of my own blood was gone for ever. It was the experience of a partial death, as we were both born Christian and consequently believed in the after-life. One of us had freed his soul from the imprisonment of the body, the other still had his earthly term to finish. I remained deeply shocked, and my grief drove me to search for all that remained of my youth, from dusty family albums of photographs, neglected on a bookshelf for many years, to the many relatives for so long unseen.

This desire to see more of my relatives prompted me to accept an invitation to a family gathering at one of their feudal properties in the flat, rugged region between Rome and Civitavecchia. The bonds of consanguinity were quickly re-established in shared memories, and I was happy to meet some cousins whom I had seen only as infants when our proud parents exchanged our photographs for Christmas.

Although their family seat has been in Rome for the past three hundred years, there is nothing Roman about them. Originally bankers from Lombardy, it was a priest, Innocenzo Odescalchi, who gave them glory when in 1676 he ascended the throne of Peter as Innocent XI. One of the great Popes in history, austere and authoritarian, his generous financial assistance enabled the Austrians to fight the infidel Turks. He confronted Louis XIV over the increasing intractability of the Gallic Church, refusing to ordain as bishops many candidates selected by the king. Despite being head of the Catholic Church he supported the anti-French policy of William III. There were other remarkable

Castello Odescalchi, Palo.

personalities among the descendants, but the earlier dynamism lost its force. In the past half-century the family have led a more retired life, taking care of their properties, enjoying shooting and hunting, no longer involved in disruptive political issues – unlike their ancestors.

Our visits to my cousins' estate on the Mediterranean became more and more frequent, until finally we rented for our lifetime a small villa which stood by itself between the border of the park and a stretch of maquis that meets the sea. They would once hunt stags here, but it is now a quiet refuge where the remaining deer graze undisturbed. Although our new home could not be remotely compared with its predecessor on the Appian Way, we nevertheless felt comfortable there and enjoyed the seclusion, which encouraged my tendency at that time to withdraw from people and from the musical world as the result of my brother's death.

The youngest of the cousins, Guido, my junior by twelve

176

Guido (left) and Ladislao Odescalchi.

years, is my landlord. He lives in an elegantly converted farmhouse with a wide view over the sea, within easy walking distance from ours. He leads a comfortable life but seems a somewhat solitary figure, and his uncertain health inclines him to pessimism. He rarely travels – I have the impression that he is never as happy in any foreign country as in his own.

The proximity of our houses encourages a close relationship based on affection and affinity. I, being the eldest of the cousins living in the neighbourhood, and being considered the 'Maestro', was not expected to pay the regular calls: instead the others came, and still come, to us in the late afternoon for a whisky or a vodka. We pass the time happily talking about music, playing records, or chatting about politics. In the morning we walk for an hour through the park of the Castle of Palo, which belongs to Ladislao, another cousin. The castle was built around one of the many medieval towers dotting the Tyrrhenian coast to defend the Italians from Saracen invasion. The present structure, whose

Palo: Nena and the villa.

origins can be traced back to the early eleventh century, was for some time Pope Leo X's hunting lodge. The massive outer wall is breached by a handsome archway by Sangallo. It was from the Castle of Palo, according to legend, that Queen Christina left for Sweden.

My wife and I share some intellectual dislikes. One of them is the profound antipathy we both have for the early works of Verdi. For an Italian who since his childhood has been exposed to that music which imbues the very air that he breathes, it is most unusual. My mind tells me that he is one of the greatest geniuses of the history of opera, but my heart is at variance with my head.

In my early youth I was taken by my parents to Sunday matinées at the Opera and Verdi was the staple diet. Sixty years ago in Florence there was little choice. When I grew older I went through practically all his operas at the piano, and it is not for want of trying if Violetta's death did not break my heart.

In later years, when I had my first job at the Opera House in Florence, I went so far – when my presence was not needed – as to vanish into the canteen for a cup of coffee in order not to hear the jolly *Allegro con brio* when Gilda rushes into her father's arms in *Rigoletto*, or the gypsies beating hell out of the anvils in the chorus of the Zingarella in *Trovatore*. I always made my reappearance for the 'Miserere' which has a spectacular theatrical effect. If I am unmoved by the often banal tunes, I am occasionally transported by the masterly handling of the dramatic elements in the plot. What could be more stirring than the quartet in *Rigoletto's* last act, Desdemona's death scene, the harassing 'Dies Irae' in the *Requiem,* or the impending doom one feels in the first bars of the *Sicilian Vespers* overture?

A musical stain on my conscience is a performance of *Aïda* in English which I conducted in Australia. Verdi is untranslatable. The expression of the Italian words and the phonetic impact of the language is so much a part of the music and the drama that a translation can only enfeeble the effect. Verdi's punctiliousness in searching for the right words to fit the music became an obsession with his librettists, Francesco Maria Piave and Salvatore Cammarano.

Toscanini's sense of grandeur and eloquence led him to be Verdi's greatest interpreter. He took infinite pains to teach the singers the enunciation of the words. While rehearsing *Aïda*, I recall his demand that the priests should over-emphasise, in the scene of the Temple, the consonant 'm' in 'Immenso Phta'. He shouted to the chorus 'Not two "m"'s, but a hundred "m"'s!' to project the immense power of the Egyptian God. The English translation is 'Almighty Phta', a rather weak-sounding word to convey boundlessness. And one can never forget the chilling effect Toscanini obtained in the *Requiem* just before the final fugue by over-pronouncing the 'r's in the whispered 'Libera me Domine de morte aeterna in diae illa tremenda'.

Verdi relies on the sound of the word to complement the music; at times, however, one cannot help feeling that the word has been chosen for its sound rather than for its sense. No better words can be found than 'Stride la vampa!' in *Trovatore*, but I have yet to discover who was Manrico's mother. The story is very complicated, and to attempt to give the reader an explanation requires an exegesis more arduous than the interpretation of Dante's most difficult passages in the *Divina Commedia*. Nevertheless, which of the two infants was roasted by the pyre in *Trovatore* is ultimately unimportant. Verdi wanted lively action, unexpected incidents and cared little if the plot was largely impenetrable. What is essential is the shattering drama, the grandiloquence of his over-charged characters, because his virile music has the nineteenth-century spirit of the Risorgimento Italiano – one can hear the drums and clarions of his passionate revolutionary genius. How could I reconcile my inborn reserve with so much force combined with such freely expressed emotions?

As I have reached an age when the past is definitely much longer than the future, I feel that it is about time to put my thoughts in order, to assess many things that I have overvalued and others that I have underestimated.

I have never tried to follow a pattern through my life, or to impose on myself a career planned from a beginning through a successful middle age to an eventually glamorous end. I have always lived very much in the present, and I have welcomed comfort and luxury, provided I did not have to sacrifice my values, principles and integrity. I have never liked a Bohemian way of life. I have paid my bills promptly, I have hated to be in debt, and as soon as I could afford it, I settled wherever I was in a comfortable lodging and pleasant surroundings, preferably in the country. I made music for my own satisfaction, an organic need that originated in my early youth, and I have enjoyed the pleasures of life without suffering the frustration that stems from vanity. I have often wondered about the happy fate that determined my career, and at the unlucky chances that occasionally halted the evolution of success.

Many things in which I was taught to believe have been radically transformed. My generation felt it had to rush through adolescence to overcome the disadvantages of youth and to acquire the experience which forms maturity, whereas today's young musicians are ready to face a career at an early age. They are competent, self-assured and unrestrained by convention; they can afford to travel cheaply to distant countries, and can learn a great deal through recordings. In my youth we had to gain knowledge as best we might. We learned with inferior orchestras, rehearsing and devising how to solve difficult technical passages unaided, while simultaneously discovering ourselves.

Nowadays a young conductor is immediately paired with a first-class orchestra through which to express his interpretative gifts, if he has any. For a composer the stave used for centuries in manuscript music is no longer always necessary. Today's writing can be in geometrical form, or in vague suggestions for free improvisation. I do not know whether the present generation, enjoying the advantages of the modern world and rapidly absorbing so much without the pains of long apprenticeship, will eventually be the poorer for missing the slow continuous growth of experience. At a mature age you appreciate life differently from when you are young. You seldom do anything you do not feel like doing; you benefit from a freedom of spirit which permits you to say whatever pleases you within the limits of the law. As I have never been malicious, and have been selfish enough not to be interested in other people's doings, I have not suffered from jealousy. On the contrary, I have been pleased by the success of people who I thought deserved it.

Although I was never the type of artist who demands that his name should be printed in large letters, or his photographs published in fashionable magazines, I was nevertheless curious to read what the papers said about my performances. I always found it perfectly normal when I was praised, and considered stupid, unfair, incompetent, and biased the critic who did not speak well of me. In my youth I was anxious to impress an orchestra at rehearsals, a weakness that troubles all young conductors. I was delighted if I could detect a false note during a torrential *fortissimo*, or display an indestructible physical endurance, or show off such memory that I could rehearse without the need for a score. Now I am indifferent to all these unnecessary things which conductors in their youth consider very important. An advantage of old age is that most of the players are younger than I am, and I do not have to hear the usual questions from the first desk, 'With Mengelberg, with Toscanini, with Furtwängler, I used to phrase it this way . . . Do you want it differently?'

If in my youth I was always pressed for time, I now face the ironic fact that at my present age I have more time than ever before. In the past I was always in a hurry to go to rehearsals. As soon as I stepped onto the podium, my baton flashed like lightning on the first chord, so as not to waste one second of the time allowed by the musicians' union. I used to repeat the same passage many times, I was nervous and excitable if my wishes were not quickly satisfied. I rushed my tempi, consequently spoiling the gradual progression to the culminating climaxes. Finally, for lack of time, I never enjoyed the pleasure of dreaming, musing, discovering.

As one grows older, one no longer cares about the impression one makes on people; one acquires a sort of take-it-or-leave-it attitude which gives assurance and conviction. When I face an orchestra now, I do not mind what they think of me as a conductor; I never open my reservoir of experience to show off what I have accumulated in the past sixty years. I talk as little as possible and I rely on my baton alone to communicate my feelings.

Quite recently I conducted a well-known European orchestra which I remembered from the past was touchy and unruly. As

rheumatism in a knee-joint prevented me from walking nor-
mally, at the first rehearsal I moved slowly down the aisle
between the first and second violins in order to reach the rostrum
and sit on my stool. They were already tuned and completely
silent. I had time to observe one by one the faces of the hundred
men in front of me, to notice that several young ones had taken
the place of some who had retired, and to recognise many
players with whom I had worked in the past, now looking
comical as if they had disguised themselves as old men to play a
joke on me. I eventually lifted my baton to start the *pianissimo*
introduction to the symphony (Tchaikovsky's Sixth), stopped at
the end of the second bar, and shook my head. I repeated the
same passage five times until I obtained a barely audible sound. I
felt then that the orchestra was keyed up and I never stopped
again until the symphony ended, because they were interpreting
my wishes without my having to explain anything.

With age we become more and more reluctant to talk to others
about our emotions; we retire increasingly into the world we
have built for ourselves. On various occasions I have been asked
if I would like to resume the intense activity I used to have up
until six years ago. I invariably answer no. I have made the best I
could of my life, I feel a growing indifference to and detachment
from the invidious factions into which the professional musical
world is divided. I now need time to improve myself. As there is
no modern music that excites my interest, I revert to the study of
works on which I have bestowed so much love and attention in
the past. I may now be able to do them greater justice. I felt that
life was escaping me and being wasted by conventional engagements and programmes that gave me little inner satisfaction.

My interest in religion has been a traditional one, the legacy of
a Roman Catholic family, and I am free from complexes of a
spiritual nature. We were all born Catholics, and Catholicism
was our way of life. I have never been a fanatical churchgoer or a
desperate worker for a future life in heaven. I was always a
believer in God and in an after-life. The past years have led to a

desire to give more sense to my temporal life, to review my old affections, to understand mankind, to guard against bitterness and disillusionment. I continue travelling and seeing people and occasionally conducting. But now I fulfil these activities in a new light, and not for professional reasons of career or as social duties. At times I feel ill at ease in the world of today, although I have no plans for leaving it. I am fundamentally a traditionalist by nature. Culture has its roots in the past, and I believe that an artist has the utmost responsibility to preserve its attainment through his own high standards. I have always borne in my mind a saying by Sir Isaac Newton: 'If I have seen further, it is by standing on the shoulders of giants.'

In the last few years my musical engagements have been undertaken for principally sentimental reasons. Monte Carlo is the place where I have conducted most often, because Renzo Rossellini was the artistic director. When I conducted in Rome for the first time in the early Thirties, with the Budapest Symphony, Renzo was the music critic of the *Messagero* and wrote an enthusiastic review of the concert. We met shortly after and became friends. I also knew and liked his brother Roberto, though they were quite different. Renzo was calm and sedate, dedicated to music – a conventional acolyte of the French School; Roberto on the other hand, according to the family, was a scatterbrain, squanderer, gambler and Bohemian, a young man who would never accomplish anything. As it turned out, when I returned to Italy after the war Roberto was at the peak of his worldwide celebrity after the release of his outstanding film *Roma, Città Aperta*, and in the midst of his volcanic romance with Ingrid Bergman, whom he later married.

The Rossellinis came from a typical Roman family, with a caustic sense of humour and great theatricality. So my visits to Monte Carlo were happy reunions with Renzo, filled with laughter. I enjoyed his agile mind and his wit. He used to embroider on the description of his family. I remember him grumbling that Roberto's ex-mistress Anna Magnani had just died and Roberto had made arrangements for her to be buried with the Rossellini family. 'If he goes on like this, there'll be no room for me,' said Renzo. 'What does he think it is – a hotel?'

For four consecutive years I accepted some concerts with the Juilliard Orchestra in New York, not only because of the pleasure it gave me to conduct a splendid group of young musicians but because it also gave me a chance to be with old friends – its admirable president, Peter Mennin, and his wife Georgeanne, Ella Brailowsky, Leo and Frankey (Gershwin) Godowsky, Brian and Eleanor Ahearne, Nika Tucci, and Dorle Jarmel Soria, who had first helped me over my American début with the New York Philharmonic in 1938 and was always ready with knowledgeable advice. In 1981 I conducted the Rundfunk Orchestra in Vienna because the performances were held in the Musikverein Saal where in my youth I had had so many emotional experiences. And because I have always admired the Royal Air Force I conducted concerts in 1983 and 1986 for the RAF Benevolent Fund with the Royal Philharmonic in the Festival Hall.

In the autumn of 1986 I conducted two other concerts with the London Philharmonic because I had made my English début with them at the Festival Hall thirty-two years before. Only a few of the original players were left; even my friend Eric Bravington, the manager of the orchestra, had already died.

In June 1986 my wife and I were dining at the Connaught Hotel with Wanda and Volodia Horowitz on the night before his departure for a concert tour in Japan. We were talking of old times, the great concerts conducted by Toscanini, his generosity, his willingness to help organisations in need, and his devotion to the Casa Verdi, founded by the composer for the benefit of musicians in 1889 – Verdi built the *palazzo* for it, endowed it with a fund, and assigned his royalties to it. We all thought it would be wonderful if a concert could be given in London the

Wanda Toscanini Horowitz and MF, London, 1977.

following year to commemorate the thirtieth anniversary of the Maestro's death. I said that naturally I should be very happy to conduct it and that the work performed should be Verdi's *Requiem*. Wanda agreed. It was decided that the proceeds should go to the Casa Verdi and the Musicians Benevolent Fund.

The Memorial Concert for Arturo Toscanini was performed on 15 June 1987 in the Royal Albert Hall in the presence of the Princess of Wales. The Philharmonia Orchestra, with an ensemble of 450 voices – the London Philharmonic Choir, the Brighton Festival Chorus and the London Choral Society, with Elisabeth Connell, soprano, Diane Curtis, mezzo-soprano, Dennis O'Neill, tenor, and Nikita Storojev, bass, as soloists – were the forces under my direction. It was a memorable success. I was pleased with the achievement and happy to have been able to contribute to the memory of Toscanini and to a cause that had been so close to his heart.

MF in action, photographed by John Phillips.

Yehudi Menuhin and MF, 1990.   MF *with Jascha Heifetz, New Orleans.*

MF, stepdaughter Maria Luisa de Almagro, and Nena, 1952.

Index

Folio numbers in italic signify illustrations